A Matter of Time

Without Jesus, one is truly paralysed

By Christine Clamp

First Edition 2023

Scripture references are taken from
The Holy Bible,
New International Version

DEDICATIONS

I dedicate this book to my daughter and son, Emma and Alex, whom I love very much and mean a great deal to me. They have seen it all, and have done brilliantly and amazingly well. They have had their own life's journey to live and cope with. They have coped with their Mum and Dad's marriage break down and the change of schools, home and learning to live with their step-dad, which is never easy with a blended family. But I am so, so proud of them in what they have achieved and become.

Emma and Alex, I hope you can see and understand what I have faced on the inside and I want to share with you what God means to me and what He can be to you.

To Martyn, my husband, who has been there and stood by me and taught me to talk things through. You have made me laugh and cry as well as focusing on where God is in all this. I love you always.

To all my brothers and sisters *and* in-laws; - Paul and sister-in- law Chris II, Dave and sister-in-law Chris III, Ruth and brother- in-law Will (who sadly passed away 14th February 2017), Eunice, Ann and brother-in-law Andy, Steve and sister-in-law Cherrie, Tim, and sister-in-law Rosi, Mark and sister-in-law Wilhelmina, Sue and brother-in-law Jem and Andy and sister- in-law Kate. You are all lovely and special, you drop everything for each other and anyone.

Thank you Paul, Dave and Chris III, Ann Steer and Eunice for helping to put details together in this book as have many others too.

A special thank you to Eunice especially while I was living with her, for putting up with me, my weird ways, for being there and driving all those miles each time she came to visit me in hospital as well as picking up Emma and Alex for visiting times. Also, for the experience of living with her in Thailand for three months – a very precious time. Also, thank you for encouraging and helping me to write this book.

Thank you too Ann who came into hospital and cared for me, with her "nurses' hat" on. And Ruth and Will for travelling frequently to Frenchay and washing my clothes and sending e-mails. Thank you to Sue for visiting me as well as sharing picking up Emma and Alex for visits too.

Thank you to Jennifer Rees Larcombe who has inspired me and encouraged me in writing this book. She has been a friend of Martyn's family for many years. A very dear, special lady.

To my Mum and Dad who taught us so much and gave us the gift of knowing Jesus. Mum passed away 7th May 2008 and Dad 29th August 2016 – both at Home in Heaven, with Jesus.

FORWARD

Reading Chris's book was a deeply enjoyable experience for me. She has an intriguing way pulling her readers into her world without using quantities of unnecessary words. I felt I too was crammed into her little house which bulged to hold 11 children and two overworked and stressed-out parents. Chris introduced me to each of her brothers and sisters and made them live for me. Her father's terrible bouts of bad temper were subtly explained away in a few well-chosen words about his childhood trauma.

I lived with her through her troubled years as a teenager, imagined her pain as her first marriage disintegrated and sat with her in A and E while doctors struggled to diagnose her terrifying and very rare medical condition. This is a highly readable book and if you enjoy it only half as much as I did you will have a great treat coming your way.

Jennifer Rees Larcombe
22.09.2022

(Sadly, Jennifer passed away 24th October 2022 before I could publish this book. I am thankful to her for giving me the time she had in latter days. She will be greatly missed not just by me but many, many other people).

Well, what can I say about this lady, Chris Clamp. When Boaz used to play football there was a guy who used to stand at the side of the pitch and say "that center back, he is what it says on the tin." I didn't really get it at first and then I got it the second time. Chris Clamp is what it says on the tin. A Matter of Time is definitely a time to reflect, to encourage, to lift up, to build up and also to give faith – a faith to the faithless world that we live in; we have come across a lot of people every day who throw the towel in, not only is Chris supporting us, my name is Gram Seed and I run Sowing Seeds Ministries with Natasha Seed, my wife; but not only has she helped us by doing tireless walks and sponsor events with Martyn, her husband, but she's also prayed for many people encouraged many people and then finally wrote this book. I would advise and encourage anyone who is feeling down, low and wants to give up to read a Matter of Time. You know, time is our greatest worry at time because there's not enough time or we want time to walk quick, now let me tell you the greatest weapon we have against time is patience. Chris Clamp has had to be patient.

My name is Gram Seed, Sowing Seeds Ministries founder with my wife Natasha Seed. Please read this book and enjoy it.

www.sowingseeds.org.uk

INTRODUCTION

This is my story that I would like to share with you. When I think back to my childhood days, I visualise them as if I were looking back in my Mum's black and white photo albums. In a way I think of those days as cold and sad but atmospheric with a great deal going on behind the scenes.

It has been a hard journey with a large number of ups and downs and if you can identify with some of my experiences, I hope you won't feel isolated but you will know that you are not on your own. If you are a T.M. (Transverse Myelitis) sufferer yourself please don't feel this is the end of your life – there IS hope and please remember that you are not on your own.

It was hard at times being in a family of 13 but there were good memories too and although I and others were scared of Dad, I don't want you to feel exasperated or angry with him, he had a lot on his plate and still he loved us, he tried his best for us and he certainly mellowed as he got older. I have forgiven him, of course.

Journey with me through my memoirs of growing up in a small house with Mum and Dad and 11 children. Facing going out into the big world and coping with what it expects you to be and do. Getting married was an enormous pressure that came from society in those days and I was desperate to get married and not be left behind. But also, situations and circumstances are thrown at you out of the blue, things that you didn't see coming at all. You have to learn to live with these hurdles; how to get over or around them. One thing I have learnt (from Ruth) is that there is always HOPE. "The rainbow comes after a storm."

I have omitted a great deal regarding my first marriage, simply because I don't want to upset Emma and Alex.

I pray that you will see how much God loves us even when we mess up; He loves us enough to pay the penalty of sin with a huge price – the life of His Son, Jesus – and that you will learn how much Jesus is ready to forgive us and be at your side too.

Comments From My Siblings

Paul Burden: "Thank you for putting your experience down on paper. It is a privilege to have been able to read it"

Dave Burden: "Your book's a gripping piece, beautifully put together! It was a real treat for me, and will be for others, I'm sure."

Ruth Hooper: "Wow! Wow! Wow! Chris, you have done a wonderful job - now the world can read your story and learn!!! Thanks for sharing - what an honour!!"

Eunice Burden: "Well done Chris for being disciplined enough to write things down. When I started to read it I couldn't stop – even though I know the ending.

I love the way you covered life at 492 so vividly, as I read I had to smile at some of the memories it brought up for me.

Thanks for letting me be part of your life, I have been honoured to have had a front seat occasionally, though being in Thailand for much of your life's events I have only been a distant support.

I applaud you as I have seen you fight and overcome so many obstacles in life, not just TM but loneliness, depression, confusion and loss.

I am so sorry for the times when you have felt that I wasn't very understanding or compassionate, which I know could had added to your stress, but God has done amazing miracles in your life and the person you are and have become is glorifying and pleasing to him for sure."

Ann Nicholas: "Well Chris, you have such a good memory and ability to transfer them into the written word. I didn't realise the age gap between us would make a difference on how we grew up! Six and a half years doesn't seem that far apart when we are at the age we are now, but I think they did when we were children. Thanks for enlightening me! And giving me more insight into how life was like being one of the younger ones.

The journey of your more adult life and certainly when the Transverse Myelitis arrived, can only be admired and it's with great gratitude to Father God that you have come through it, not only physically, although I know you still have your challenges but also spiritually. In a way, it was an opportunity for Father God to let you know how amazing His unconditional love is. It's beautiful to look back on your journey and see what could have been meant for bad, God turned it around for good.

However, the journey isn't over yet!! I look forward to hearing more of Gods' amazing goodness to you in the coming years".

Steve Burden: "First Part: I Really enjoyed this section. Even though I still have issues with the whole evangelical nature of our upbringing, I thought you gave a very fair account of the 492 vibes. Amongst the rough and tumble of so many siblings sharing what was a small, cramped, end-of-terraced house, there were elements that were secure, even happy! I found myself smiling at some of the more charming incidents. Your specific memories faithfully capture a way of life that is now so dated as to seem very quaint and old fashioned. I acknowledge this was a lot of work and is a job very well done!!

Second Part: This, again, was an awful lot of work! Dealing with issues like this is very tough to read about - I can only imagine how much tougher it was to live through. Not a comfortable journey for you and I am sorry I didn't fully know the weight of stress, worry and pain of it all. Sometimes life is simply reduced to not dying! When it is in slow motion the pain lingers longer and leaves its heavy imprint on our souls.

My medical grasp of the details is so very shallow I am at a loss to comment on the content with any sense of context, knowledge or even encouragement. Clearly, one very good thing was Martyn's timely stage entrance! Well done that man!!"

Tim Burden: "I felt for you in the lonely years. I am sad not to have been of help."

Mark Burden: "Having pain as a lifelong companion, reading your book, it shows how pain can, all of sudden, makes this terrible 'entrance' if you like; I forgot just how crippling pain can be. I have before now laid in bed trying to fall asleep but I can't because everything, everything is screaming pain at you and you shown here how you have seen God's providence when you look in the rear-view mirror, as it were. And how you have come to see God at work. Reading through Job (15th book in the Bible), poor Job, a lot of the pain he suffered was trying to defend his integrity before his, so called, comforters and yet somehow God uses pain to reign us in and bring us back to him and get our attention".

Sue Jarvis: "You have an amazing memory for details. I really shouldn't have got in that Pat O'Keefe's car that day and should have listened to you!

The account of your experience in hospital is really moving and it must have been so terrifying at the beginning. It's good that you can look back on it now and have made such a good recovery though obviously 100% would have been even better.

So glad that God has brought you through all those events and that you found such happiness with Martyn."

Andy Burden: "As I read this book, I was struck by how many details Chris had remembered about those days of growing up. It is only when putting pen to paper that the memories begin to flow. The different perspectives that people have on the same set of information or circumstances has always been a fascination to me. I've never tried to search too hard for reason or explanations, but when I have, I usually come to the same conclusions.

Thank you, Chris, for sharing your memories of growing up and finding your place in this world. It explains much about why you are the wonderful person you are.

Transverse Myelitis hit you at a time just when Emily was born. How different are the experiences of life? It seemed that during that period the right people were in the right place to help and support you. I remember that Eunice was home from Thailand and thinking that there was a reason why she was home then.

You mention a lot of people and some of them I didn't know. What is clear is that your road to recovery was paved with the prayers of many. The thought came to me of the power of prayer and the joining of God's people in prayer. There are those we know, those we don't know, have never met or will ever meet and yet we all have an interest in this long journey.

You are right that our Lord is with us all the way, thank you for reminding me".

CONTENTS

1 My Dad

Dad's parents had split up when dad was only 9 years old, after which dad had next to no contact with his mother. He lived for several years with his dad, his younger brother and grandmother. His Dad was a semi-professional footballer for Bath City. But he was also a highly respected engineer. When my dad was just 15½ he lost his dad too.

It was during the Blitz – the German bombing of the UK during World War II. Dad's brother, Len, recalls that on the 25th April 1942 his dad had put him (Len) and my dad (Euan) under the dining room table with their Gran, sitting on cushions. As dad's Dad went to the front door to see what was happening, a bomb came down on an industrial storage yard opposite their house. The blast brought down the front of their home and they were buried under the rubble. Dad's Dad was killed. When they were rescued, dad and his gran were taken to a welfare centre but it was thought that Uncle Len was dead, so he was taken to the mortuary – his first memory after the bomb was waking up in their Uncle Walt's house (the Home Guard relation who supervised their rescue).

There followed several months of dad, his brother Len and their Gran staying with relatives, including a stay of six months or so in Frome with Great Aunt Rose, a sister of Gran. Eventually, Gran rented a house in Bath, just a few doors away from the home that was destroyed by the bomb. The three settled there until 1946, when Gran's failing health meant that she was no longer able to keep a house for dad and his brother.

Later on, dad remembered the 12 months after the Blitz as having been chaotic, giving him no chance to mourn for his Dad. Dad also recognised the debt he owed for the support of, in particular, his Aunts Flo and Min, the neighbours and the folks from Longmead Gospel Hall.

Meanwhile, dad had become an apprentice at Stothert & Pitt which was a British engineering company founded in 1855 in Bath, England. It was the builder of various engineering products ranging from dock cranes to construction plant and household cast iron items. It was there that he met mum in December 1943, about two months after her Dad died. Neither of them was a Christian at the time, though they both – separately – became Christians early in 1944. By the end of 1945 dad moved into Mum's home at 4 Marina Villas as her Mum's lodger.

I think it is hard for us today to understand how anyone can cope with so many tragic things happening to such young people (mum was 18 months younger than dad), but they both took both their lives and their new-found faith seriously, as illustrated in a letter dad wrote to mum in April 1946 from a hospital bed: "*I wondered why God gave me this trouble, and then had to enter hospital. But, I think, in fact I am sure, that He has taught me many things. Yes, five years of misery are over. Five years of pain and uncertainty are gone forever, please God.*"

Dad was an electrical engineer and well respected for his area of workmanship. After a time at Stothert's he worked at Cross Manufacturing Company (1938) Ltd. in Bath. Cross's specialised in the design and manufacture of heat resisting wrought alloy sealing-rings etc. and at one point helped to make the engine rings for Concorde. Dad also went on to work for Clarks – he was in the unit for the manufacturing of the machines that make the shoes.

When we were very little there used to be Bible study meetings at our house and there seemed loads of young people who would all sit in the lounge and spill out into the hall way. I got the impression that these young people loved coming to our house and learning about the Bible, so mum and dad must have had quite a ministry and helped all these young people in their understanding of the Bible. Dad was also a 'lay-preacher' and often spoke at different churches in Bath and even as far away as a church in Crockerton, Warminster. We went to tea with a family who also had the surname 'Burden' but they weren't related to us.

Dad worked hard to keep a roof over our heads, food on the table, clothes over our shoulders and shoes on our feet. But he was stressed and had a short fuse. I think the stress of work and 13 mouths to feed was too much for dad – probably most days he was 'Burdened' down by it all. When dad gave any of us a hug, he would hold you tight but it didn't feel lovely, snuggly, soft or gentle. I would feel scared and my whole being would go as stiff as a board. Maybe he didn't know his own strength? The question is, how could any of us cope with 11 children - wouldn't we be stressed?

Dad also used to have black-outs; he would be doing something quite normal e.g., putting his slippers on one minute and the next minute he would be unconscious on the floor. For this reason, he wasn't allowed to drive and so we never had a car. But we were provided with good shoes so walking everywhere wasn't a problem, although the more you walked the more pairs of shoes you needed and don't grow too quickly! Or we could use public transport which was easy enough to use because we had a bus stop right outside in the lay-by.

I really don't think dad could manage with the responsibility of us all. Even if mum and dad had one more child it would not have been 'cheaper by the dozen'! I was scared of dad. I thought that if I knew where he was in the house, I was safe. If he got angry and raised his voice I would freeze and tremble. Forgiveness is a precious thing. As the years went by, dad did mellow and he was proud of us all and loved us all very much.

2 My Mum

My mum was a lonely child, no brothers and sisters. Her parents weren't Christians themselves but her dad was always searching for the truth and her Mum would pray that her daughter "would grow up to be a real Christian and marry a real Christian man." But Gran (my mums' Mum) did not know what it meant to be a real Christian. When mum's Dad became very ill, before he died, he said "I give myself into His hands" and his face lit up with joy! He said "It's alright! There's no pain now! If only I'd known before! Tell everyone it's alright." He must have seen heaven before he passed away and he realised that we don't have to earn a place to get to heaven, only believe and trust in the Lord Jesus Christ to be saved. How amazing is that – to have that astonishing revelation before dying. This experience led Gran and mum to become believers too.

Mum went to an art school in Bath but had to leave when she was young to find a job when her dad was so unwell because they had little income. But she never lost her artistic talent. She loved painting which she did more of in her later years.

Because mum was an only child, she made up for lack of company with all eleven of us! But it was a busy life. Mum was always somewhere in the house doing something or hanging up the washing in the garden. I don't think she really enjoyed cooking but she loved doing the washing. It was something she could organise and work through and she was brilliant at it. It was a big task and must have been very rewarding for her to get it all done, she also had help from us at different stages of our lives.

There was the ironing, of course. To me, as a small child, it seemed like steep mountains of the stuff. Saturday was the main washing day – mum must have felt like a Victorian Washer Woman at times or a Chinese Laundry!

Mum was brilliant when you weren't well. She was up and down those stairs like a yo-yo. She would regularly check on you or get the doctor to come if we were poorly. Drinks were on 'tap', the room ventilated and extra blankets were found if you had the shivers and a bucket available if you had a bad tummy bug.

When I was ill (which was often as a child), I remember sitting on mum's lap and snuggling up to her and it was simply bliss if she kissed me on the top of my head. It was a great sense of security. I loved those moments. Sadly, they didn't last and as I grew older, I realised that I couldn't have a cuddle when I wanted one because she would say 'not now, I'm busy'. This was hard to swallow, it was like being left behind, standing there on your own. But I understood that she was busy and at a young age we all accepted that things were the way they were just because we were a big family.

She worked hard making ends meet. Sometimes she couldn't afford to give us 'pocket money' which was half your age in old Shillings and Pence. So, when I was six, I remember that my 'pocket money' was 3d (today that would be worth 1.25p = 1 and a quarter pence). Mum had an orange tin box that had slots for you to put money in and under the lid you could see that the coins would fall into different sections in the tin box. She would save so much for the weekly shop, some for clothes/shoes and so on. It was her budget box and this is something I adopted when the money was short and my daughter also uses this idea. Thanks mum!

Mum was often the go-between in any disagreements, especially when it was between dad and any of us children. Mum understood the stress that dad was under but she also saw things from our point of view. She could have done with a referee's outfit and a whistle on occasions!

3 Our Family

I was number 9 out of a family of 11 children. It is only in my more recent years that I have learnt not to think of myself as number 9 but as Chris (or Christine).

I love my brothers and sisters very much and we are a close family. We keep in contact really well and we have zoom to thank for that. **Paul** was born July 1949 (after being a teacher he worked at the British Library). He is the eldest and he went off to university before I really got to know him. When I did see him, he seemed serious all the time, but actually I now know him as the one who is sensitive and can laugh very easily and has a lovely giggle.

Then there's **Dave** born January 1951 (he became a computer analyst). He is very quiet, a man of few words, gentle and loves listening to classical music. Dave had a lovely musical box which I adored to listen to and, for some reason, Dave liked Noddy!?

Ruth was born July 1952 (now, a Trusts and Foundations Fundraiser for Designability) - I always feel loved by Ruth and she's like a Mum to me, making me feel secure too. She is very selfless and would do anything for anyone. I used to think she was very tall when I was young, and very pretty. She is still pretty, of course, but not as tall as I remember. It was probably because I was so small.

Eunice was born in March 1954 (now, a missionary in Thailand). She wanted to be a doctor originally but became a Laboratory technician for a while and other jobs before going to Bible College. She would always say that she was the 'black sheep' of the family. But she was never black or furry but always full of life and adventure, laughed loads and loudly, always had something funny to say, she is also a real servant of God.

Ann arrived in May 1955 and is the nurse of the family. She trained in different areas of nursing. Ann is very neat and tidy and she used to have long, wavy hair and under her bed, in a box, she used to have costume dolls and I broke the arm off one of them because Ann wouldn't give me a polo mint – so sorry Ann!

Steve who was born September 1956 (now, a piano tuner). He used to have hair down to his shoulders and spots as a teenager. Today, he is very smart, smiles loads and has a lovely chuckle.

Tim who arrived January 1958 (he became a pastor). He was good at math's, football and tech drawing and was employed at Stothert and Pitt before going to Bible College. Steve and Tim always seemed to come together as two best mates and I always used to look up to them. I wanted to climb the tree like them and tackle the ball with them when playing football.

Mark was born 1961 (who is one year older than me) and I always used to hold his hands but I don't really remember those days but there are photographs to prove it. He became a diabetic at the age of three from a virus which changed his whole life. He learnt to inject himself with insulin and later on I remember him trying to teach me to inject him in case of an emergency – I didn't like doing it! He loved his Airfix model planes (and still does!) and his little, green, plastic soldiers, tanks, trains and cars. Mark also worked at Stothert and Pitt but later went into restoring Antique Clocks but ill-health caught up with him and he takes one day at a time.

Then I was born, November 1962, I loved drawing and dreaming out the window!

Two years later **Sue** (Susanna) arrived, November 1964. She was cute, pretty, very popular at school and intelligent. She did well at school and worked for Herman Miller for a while.

Now Sue works at Bath University – she's very on the "ball" with a lovely sense of humour. I remember Sue asking mum to pray for a brother or sister and Mum said 'well, we'll see what we can do shall we?'. Then Andy appeared 9 months later in July 1968 and what a cute one he was!

Andy is fun, caring and loving and he surely has more than enough brains for just one person! He started learning to play the piano at aged six! Andy did well at math's and now works for the M.O.D. but I have no idea what he does there!

4 492

As a family, we always refer to our home as 492 because it was the number of the house. We lived on the main road going out of Bath; if you continued on the same road, you would eventually arrive at Exeter. Our house was the last house in a row of four other houses next to a lay-by and a bus stop. The four houses used to be called Marina Villas and our house was No. 4.

The area of Bath that we lived in was called Odd Down. The area was given its name by the Saxons – **Odda's Hill,** but in English it means Odd Down. Being at the top of one of the hills going out of Bath it was always very windy or very hot in the summer.

We used to have a wooden gate until Dad changed it to an iron gate. With all the swinging, back and forth it obviously became very squeaky. The green front door was wooden but very secure and once you have stepped inside you were standing in the hallway, the dining room was on your right. I seem to remember an electric 3 bar fire which was later replaced by a gas fire. There was a piano just behind the door and a bookcase in the left-hand corner of the room. But mainly, the room was taken up with a large table, several chairs and a wooden blanket box which was used as a bench at meal times. Sometimes meals were in two sittings and later we had a small table which the 'grown ups' were allowed to sit at.

At meal times you weren't allowed to speak so we ate in silence because mum and dad were born in the era of 'children should be seen and not heard.' We had small portions and if you ate your meals like Eunice it was gone in seconds. Mum often berated Eun for gulping her food down! Mum would cook a cottage pie, which was my favourite, with a pound of mincemeat and it had to stretch between us all. The vegetables came from dad's vegetable patch in the garden. We had carrots, runner beans, broad beans, cabbage, lettuce, potatoes and tomatoes in the greenhouse at the bottom of the garden. Otherwise, if it was out of season, we would have tinned carrots or peas. Sometimes we had sausages, lamb chops, fish fingers, casserole or a stew. We also had a large cooking apple tree which supplied us well with apple crumble or apple pie, I was never keen on baked apple though.

On Sundays, we always had a roast dinner. Mum cooked a small beef or lamb or chicken in the 'green roasting tin'. The meat depended on which was cheaper at the time. Our dessert would be a cup of tea and Custard Cream or Bourbon biscuits. Sadly, this didn't do our teeth any good and only enhanced our 'sweet teeth'!

The hallway, dad had painted the banisters orange and there was a diamond, floral type wall paper. It was certainly bold and bright! Maybe the orange paint was cheaper or he thought all the dirty hand prints wouldn't show up so much; who knows? The stairs and hallway flooring, as I remember it, had red "lino". Good for all those little feet running up and down on it.

Exit the dining room, turn right and the lounge was next. Just inside the lounge door dad had to screw a panel of veneer wood, simply because several of us used to pop our heads round the door to see what was going on, who was in there, who was missing or what was on the television so we wore a grey patch on the wall (our viewing area). The panel at least protected a large square area! There were a couple of single arm chairs, a long stool, a small stool as well as a maroon covered settee which could be pulled out to make a double bed. It probably wasn't very comfortable because we jumped and did somersaults on it so much it must have got out of shape. Its vocation should have been a trampoline!

We had a coal fire in the lounge a Parkray fire. This was used to heat the lounge and hot water (immersion heater). I remember being up early one morning, in the winter, watching dad light the fire and getting ready to walk to work. He was whistling ('What shall we do with the drunken sailor?') and cheerfully putting on his shoes in the warmth of the lounge. I was gazing with fascination at the flames catching fire to the paper and wood, then lighting up different pieces of coal. The glass door was open and I felt the heat on my face – it was wonderful to feel so very warm that I didn't want to move away because the heat felt so amazing. As I stared at the flames I began to question, how do flames work? Dad had left the house by now and I was still intrigued with this fire. I'm not sure whether it was this occasion or a different one but there was an incident when I put my hands in the fire and blistered them – I'll never do that again. (I was three when this happened).

The next room was the kitchen where dad fixed a sliding door to make more room. We had a small cooker. It was a 1950's G.E.C. Electric Cooker. Mum was later treated to a Belling Cooker which had a timer on it – mum loved the timer! We had a basic sink and draining board, a kitchen stool which stood next to the cooker by the doorway with the ironing board and we had a trolley on the left of the room, which added an extra surface area. Immediately on the left of the doorway was a cupboard, which was part of the cupboard under the stairs area and this had hats, bags, scarfs and gloves – loads of them! I also think the hoover lived in that cupboard too. Then, if you swiveled to your right there was a built-in wooden shelf come cupboard. Plates, saucers, bowls and hooks for cups and mugs, the first aid box, tea, coffee and sugar storage jars, scrap paper for shopping lists etc. lived on these shelves. At the bottom it had a cupboard where the shoe polish, dusters, dustpan and brush and cleaning fluids were kept. The shoe polish and brushes were in a biscuit tin and everyone – I mean everyone – had to learn how to polish their own shoes. Preferable to be done on a Saturday so that they were clean and shiny for church and ready for the week ahead.

If you turned left at the trolley you came into the Little Kitchen or Little Room. I have a feeling that dad continued with the orange décor in this room as well. But in here was a large side board cabinet with table cloths, saucepans, baking tins, cooking utensils, plastic bowls and a drawer of cutlery. There was a pantry full of jams, sauces etc. On the very top shelf was a cardboard box which was called the Sunday Box. This had chocolate biscuits in, trifle mixes, blocks of jelly and cake mixes – all the lovely sweet tasting treats for a tasty Sunday tea!

Along the inner wall was a light green kitchen cabinet that people had in their kitchens in the 1950's. It consisted of a double base cupboard with an internal shelf, two drawers and a pull-down top with a Formica worktop. A lot of food preparation was done on that Formica worktop e.g. slices of bread laid out for buttering *lots* of sandwiches.

I can't remember when the fridge came into being because I remember a fridge appearing which seemed like the best thing since sliced bread! A new kitchen accessory that everyone was buying. Maybe the older ones can remember whether we had something else for the milk, cheese and ham etc.

We had a water-driven potato peeler. It was bowl shaped with a large hole at the top to drop potatoes in. It was rough inside like sand paper. But this was a brilliant invention especially if you had to peel lots of potatoes for dinner. There was a tube that you connected to the tap and tightened it with a clip. Turn the water on and the water would run down the tube and spurt out water into a 'water wheel' which in turn moved the bottom of the bowl so that the potatoes would jolly around this bowl with the 'sand paper' walls slowly peeling off the skins of the potatoes. Just turn the tap off and 'Bob's your uncle' you have peeled potatoes!! Mind you, it was a "dickens" to clean out and you still had to peel out the 'eyes' of the potatoes. Still, it meant you didn't have to peel chunks of potato peel off and it did make things easier and faster.

We all helped with preparing meals unless there were too many cooks in the kitchen. But you did learn at an early age to cook as well as clean and do the washing.

There was a back door in the kitchen, leading to a small porch and then to a lean-to greenhouse-like building which, in the winter, was *so* cold. There was another door, in the porch, right in front of you and with a latch, which I only remember as a place where the mop was and some junk and cobwebs. But it did have a toilet! At one point in our younger years, mum cleared it out and painted it and this meant we had two toilets in a family of 13! This was such a good brain storm of mum's because the queue outside the bathroom could get ridiculously long at times.

Dad had more or less rebuilt the conservatory or greenhouse as we often called it. Conservatory was a big word for us younger ones. It was freezing in winter and very hot in the summer and fantastic to dry and air the washing during those months.

Outside the conservatory were the dustbins and then the coal bunker! This was dark, dirty and very black but if we were playing hide and seek and you were feeling brave, it was an extremely good place to hide.

I remember watching Mark, climbing out of the bathroom window and down the slanting roof of the 'outside' toilet and down over the coal bunker and into the garden. This was SO daring. The first time he did it my eyes nearly popped out of my head! I did try once, I remember, but I was too scared getting out of the bathroom window onto the roof, needless to say, I didn't make it – I chickened out.

It was originally, only a three-bedroom, end of terrace build. In March 1954 an extension was built onto the house (we called it the annex); this was before I was born. This allowed a further two bedrooms upstairs and an extra-long room for the kitchen and dining area.

Gran lived with us and had the front main dining room. But as the family got bigger Gran moved to a flat next door. Mum was a cleaner & caretaker for the doctors' surgery next door to us. Gran lived in the upstairs flat (June 1966). I was four years old and just about remember the flat. One or two of us would sometime visit and have tea with her; later in the evenings Paul and Dave would say good night and go out of the house to sleep in the flat to keep Gran company, which also gave a bit more space at home. In one of the rooms, in the flat, it was big enough to lay out the whole train set. The trains went round by themselves! Not really, it was all by electric – it had a transformer box. Mark played with this train set a lot and I remember lying down next to the track and watching the carriages go by and imagining people inside it, maybe going to the seaside or visiting family in the countryside. It seemed real to me in this little model world – it was fascinating to me.

Back at home, there was a cupboard under the upstairs and it was full of shoes! If they were in a muddle, which was often the case, it was like looking for a needle in a haystack to try and find your matching shoe and it smelt of .... well... feet and worn shoes. The electric meter also lived in there and I was very thankful that dad had put a light in the cupboard otherwise I wasn't sure what else lived in there. No 'shoe monsters' anyway!

The bedrooms in the annex would have ice appear on the inside of the windows in the winter. I think this was very common for a lot of people in homes before central heating. I used to share a bedroom with Sue and Mark. Mark and I had to share a bed – Mark at one end and me at the other, which wasn't fun if you accidentally kicked each other in the night. As Paul and Dave went off to university there was more space to move around and have your own bed. Paul first left in September 1967 for a three-year teacher's training course in Exeter. Dave went to university in Durham two years later to do a similar course. So, Ruth had her own room, which we called the 'box room'; the smallest bedroom in the house. Steve, Tim and Mark had the largest bedroom, which was above the dining room. They had green, heavy metal bunk beds and as time moved on, they became very squeaky especially when climbing up the ladder end of the beds. Ann and Eunice had one of the front annex bedrooms and Sue, Andy and I had the back annex bedroom. Mum and dad, of course, had the bedroom above the lounge.

We ran out of beds at one point in our younger lives and dad made two beds out of wood with dovetail connections in the corners. A very quick and very simple design. He then put wheels on the four corners for easy mobility, and a large piece of ply wood on the top and then the mattress!

5 Living At Home

In the summer holidays we were left to play imaginary games, cricket, rounders or football between ourselves. My favourite was French Cricket because you all had a go and you didn't get bored if you were 'fielding' like in a normal game of cricket. That was one good thing about a large family – you could make up teams! Mum would send us 'over the field'. There was a playing field which was just across the road from us behind a stone wall. It saved the grass in our garden from getting worn and a muddy patch. It was very handy for us all to charge over there and run off all the energy that we had! It was a very uneven field and at times you would fall over not expecting bumps in certain areas. It wasn't until years later that I learnt that it used to be the workhouse graveyard! Maybe we should have run around the bumps in the field?

When it was tea time or we had to go back home mum would blow a whistle from the top front bedroom window! Passer-bys must have wondered what Mum was doing but to us it was the signal for home-time. We lived on a main road so it wasn't always easy to cross the road to home. You had to be careful and we often used the 'bollards' (which was in the middle of the road several houses down) as a halfway crossing site.

We often had a picnic tea in the garden. The green roasting tin had many uses and one was to fill it up with jam sandwiches with the lid on, so that the flies and wasps didn't get a look in or have a picnic for themselves. A tray loaded up with lots of cups and saucers was taken out with sugar, teaspoons, milk and a large pot of tea. There were often tasty biscuits and home-made cakes too to make it a scrummy meal time. Mum and dad had a deck chair each and usually the older ones too; the younger ones sat on the grass or a blanket as was expected.

I remember one day dad came home with a metal ring. I guess it was a reject item from what he was working on at his place of work. I knew he had been making engine rings and even made some for the first Concorde!! So, this metal ring, despite it being quite heavy became a hoop for us to play with. It was fun for a short while but it would hurt you especially if it landed on your foot.

We had rabbits and guinea pigs but I just don't remember them very well. I think Ruth had the rabbits; Ann was the one with the guinea pigs. Paul had a mouse and I am sure Eunice did too. There was a tortoise that Mum bought for tuppence, so it was called Tuppence. We had a black cat that had white paws and he was called Spotty but I remember Spotty as a bit of a vicious character. Mum asked me to feed him once so I put his tinned cat food (Kitty-Kat) on his saucer and he would try and scratch you. So, I speedily put the food down on the floor and ran!

One summer's day, Steve and Tim were playing cricket and whoever was batting missed the ball and the heavy cricket ball went flying into the lounge casement window pane. There was a sense of the boys being stunned and very worried what dad would say. With mum's help they had to use their pocket money and buy a new pane of glass and some putty and replace the broken window. I must admit they did a pretty good job – they could have become professionals! I don't think that breaking the news to dad was easy but at least they had repaired it. If they wanted to play cricket again, they had to do it away from the lounge windows and, I can't remember, but maybe they were only allowed to use a tennis ball after that!

Steve and Tim had asked to use the old pram wheels to make a 'go-cart'. Probably the pram used when Andy was a baby. It couldn't have been the toy pram as it wouldn't have been strong enough. Wherever the wheels came from they moved fast in their new roll of becoming a 'go-cart'. Steve and Tim managed to build a wooden box to sit in with a separate short plank of wood attached to the two front wheels with string attached for steering. It was fun just to run next to the cart and watch Steve and Tim try out their new invention.

Dad put a 'platform' in the apple tree in the garden. It was a large cooking apple tree and dad manage to get hold of a large piece of wood and shaped it so that it fitted in between parts of the trunk and branches to create a platform type tree house. No roof just floor space. This was exciting because it was like having a den in the tree. We took pillows or cushions up with our books or colouring books *and,* of course, plastic binoculars in case you were on the lookout for pirates! Also, in this tree, Mark, Sue, Andy and I had 'perches. The highest one was Mark's, the next one down was mine, Sue's and then Andy's near the bottom of the tree trunk. Around September we helped Mum harvest the cooking apples. We first had to pick up the fallers. Some were bruised, squidgy on one side, and some were chewed by both maggots and birds. But the best part was to then climb the tree and pick the ripe ones. If we couldn't reach from our perches then out came the ladder and stick or broom. We stewed apple, baked it or we had my favourite of apple crumble.

Once we made bows and arrows out of string and twigs. They worked really well! I got my arrow, lined it up with the string and bow, pulled back as far as I dared and then 'release' off it went and got stuck in the apple tree! I couldn't have done it if I had planned it. Robin Hood, here I come or shall I be Maid Marian?

Other times we played under the dining room table. If this was a play time before the hoovering was done, I didn't like the shriveled-up garden peas and dried up old pieces of bread and toast but it was an excellent hide-away if you were playing hide and seek or even having a teddy bears' picnic.

We had a game of 'Budge' or 'Fudge' where you had to choose several 'bases' in the garden e.g., the washing line post, the swing etc. once they were allocated as safe places someone had to be 'it' and chase us before we got to a 'base'. If you were tagged then you became 'it'. Only one person was allowed on each 'base' at a time so you could run to one 'base' and tell the sibling already there to 'budge off' or just 'budge' or even 'fudge'! We used similar rules for Off Ground Touch. You would choose 'bases' that were off ground e.g., the tree, the swing or a garden chair and off you played with the same rules.

There was a 3 wheeled scooter and, what seemed a very big adult, tricycle, a little tricycle, roller skates and an old-fashioned red pedal car to play with. I travelled many miles in that car and visited faraway places of imaginary, beautiful countryside. Unfortunately, the back garden path was as good as a cross country bumpy pathway, except the path which was alongside the annex to the back gate and garden.

We would sometimes go out for a walk on a Bank Holiday weekend and I can remember coming back from a walk (which seemed like a day of trekking to me) along the road in twos or threes or fours and a couple of cars slowed down or stopped to ask if there was something going on somewhere that they hadn't heard about or missed. Maybe they thought a crowd of us were going to some event that hadn't been well advertised! It was very amusing.

We also played board games. Some of them the older siblings played – I think one was called Contraband. I didn't understand that game. We played Ludo, Monopoly, Cluedo, Chess, draughts, Snakes and Ladders and Sorry, Snap, Pairs and the memory game. Mum had her own version of a memory game. She would come into the lounge with a tray with objects on it covered with a Tea Towel. She would give us a couple of minutes to look at them and try and remember them all. She would then cover the tray and we had to remember the articles – I hated that game – I have such a bad memory! We also had a cupboard of jigsaw puzzles, which I loved and were always a challenge.

God was obviously a big part of our growing up. Mum and dad took us to church and Sunday school every week and if you weren't well, it was hard 'to get out of going'. In the evenings, every day of the week, before bed-time we had what was known as 'family altar'. This was when we all gathered together in the lounge with our Bibles and dad would read the verse off the calendar. We then all had to read a verse of the Bible as we read the passage around the reference verse on the calendar. I didn't find this much fun because of my problem reading. After the reading we would all get up off our seat and turn round and kneel and we would go around the room, in age order, and one by one we prayed. The lounge wasn't a very big room so when we were all home together anyone peeping their head around the door during prayer time of an evening would have seen an array of slippers and bottoms in the air!

I became a Christian at the young age of three or four. I remember praying the prayer of asking Jesus into my heart with my mum. There was no flashing lights or special feelings that I experienced after that prayer. But as I grew older Jesus was my close friend. I couldn't see him but neither could I see the wind but I knew it was there, certainly on a windy day and you are so sure about it and no-one can make you doubt it. So, faith is believing in something you can't see:

1 Peter Chapter 1:8-9 (New International Version)
"8 Though you have not seen him, you love him; and even though you do not see him now, you believe in him and are filled with an inexpressible and glorious joy, 9 for you are receiving the end result of your faith, the salvation of your souls."

I could talk to Him about anything and at any time. Being a teenager in a big family wasn't easy. Sometimes I just wanted to be alone and other times I could feel really lonely, which is ridiculous. But if I hadn't had Jesus to talk to, I think I would have fallen off the top bunk bed in more ways than one!

I was a bit jealous of little Andy, so one day, I slammed the back conservatory door and rushed outside and hid by the side gate. Andy didn't like the banging of the door and burst into tears and wailed loudly. I did this about five times and then felt very bad and owned up to mum and told her why Andy kept screaming and crying out loud. She wasn't very happy with me!

I couldn't play the piano but one day I prayed (I was about five years old), sitting on the piano stall, I asked Jesus to let me play the piano – 'right now and all of a sudden please'. When I opened my eyes, I expected to be proficient with the piano keys and pour out music like I have never heard before. It was then I realised that Jesus had nothing to do with 'magic' stuff and that was just the television that made me think things happen in a puff of smoke.

Before Andy was born Mark, Sue and I played together but with three, there is often one left out. It would be either Mark and me playing or Sue and Mark or just Sue and myself. Three's not such a good number – 'three's a crowd' as they say. I remember one evening, it was still light and we were told to get ready for bed. There was only one bathroom in our home and often a queue outside on the landing, each waiting their turn. This particular evening, I was just finishing in the bathroom, I opened the door and Mark and Sue were itching to get into the bathroom for their turn. I wanted to decide who went in next and it wasn't going to be Mark! I tried closing the door but something was wrong – it wouldn't shut. Almost instantly, Sue screamed because I hadn't realised that her finger was in the door jam. I quickly ran out of the bathroom and into the bedroom but I couldn't get away from dad's wrath. We were all reprimanded for messing around at the top of the stairs and I especially for trapping Sue's finger in the door even though it was an accident. Sue's finger was, thankfully, still attached but very bruised. I felt so, so bad.

At the top of the stairs there was a couple of extra steps that turned to the left for the bedrooms in the annex. Sue and I often would meet here and think, contemplate, debate and moan. We talked about everything under the sun. We would share our feelings, our struggles and moan about the lack of pocket money, choice of clothes – the list was long. It was our way of coping – a problem shared was a problem halved. We must have worn two seating patches into the carpet on that top step and that step must have listened to lots of secrets that young girls share between each other.

As a child, I was gentle and quiet; I usually watched others and learnt from their mistakes. I cared about others and wanted to treat friends and other people as I would want to be treated. And I tried to be good even when it was hard. I was always being unwell and very pale. I often had tonsillitis and I'm sure I lived on Minadex which was a green, thick, sweet syrup full of Iron. If any one of us became ill in the home, the best thing for everyone was that you stayed out of the way in bed otherwise it would go all round the family. There was one time where one by one we all went down with a sickness bug – not good!! And another time I was off school for a week with the flu, went back to school for a day and then I was off another week with tonsillitis! Dad was really cross when he came home again because I was off sick yet again.

I loved drawing and used to draw loads especially for mum and mostly in the holidays. In the long holidays mum would often do a Drawing Competition but quite often mum couldn't decide and would make us all winners, then there would be no upsets or quarrels. If your drawing went into her box under her bed then you knew you had done a good picture. That box seemed like her treasure chest of our pictures.

At Christmas, certainly the younger you were the more excited you were. Christmas parties at school or Sunday School were so much fun and more food! We had a small Christmas tree which was put in the corner near the television, balloons were blown up and hung up as well as paper chains from corner to corner of the lounge and a white church ornament which I loved because it had a light inside and it shone through the plastic 'stained glass window' which made it very effective.

Christmas Eve night we would put one of our socks at the end of our beds and in the morning, we had an orange, a present and our favourite Annuals. For a couple of years, I would get Rupert The Bear which I couldn't understand because I didn't like him! One Christmas, both Sue and I got 'Yes and No' dolls. You would press a button on the front of her tummy and the head would nod and if you pressed the button on the back the head would move side to side.

Another Christmas I had a red watch. I loved that watch!! One year I had a blue Bible which zipped up on three sides and the edge of the pages were silver. Very smart! When I was about 6, I really wanted this plastic horse where the head would move and its knees too. I was so desperate for it that I prayed and prayed to Jesus every night for months before Christmas, even promising to be a good girl and keep my room tidy. Amazingly, it appeared on Christmas morning with a saddle included. I was so happy!

I can think of some comical cases over different Christmases. For several years running Sue and I didn't have much money to buy presents out of our pocket money but it was also not expected. However, we wanted to give presents. It was easy enough to go through our toy box and find small toys that we didn't play with anymore. We would wrap them up and proudly give out the presents to our brothers and sisters the attractively Christmas gift/toys. Once, Sue asked Tim what he wanted for Christmas and he laughed and jokingly replied a pop balloon. And what did she give him? Yes, a popped balloon all neatly wrapped up. Dad used to joke that all he wanted was a box full of peace and quiet. One year, that's what Sue gave him. A matchbox that had absolutely nothing in it and on the front, it simply said "Peace and Quiet". Well, it made dad laugh!!

What I loved about Christmas was the food! Mum and dad would order a Christmas hamper, which Dad got from a catalogue from work and it had all the Christmas goodies you could wish for. The mince pies were amazing and my sisters would make Christmas cakes in their cookery classes when they were at secondary school. Royal Icing is the best, I'm sorry, but the rolled out icing you get these days does not beat it by half. So, when the girls made their Christmas cakes it was a very special treat. Even my brother Tim, made a Christmas Cake one year with very delicate icing – it was an artist's master piece. Sadly, as soon as Boxing Day had arrived, the balloons came down and that seemed to signal the end of Christmas. All that build up for one day and all of a sudden it was all done and dusted. Although there might be some Christmas cake left over!

When I was four or five some of the older siblings left home and so there was more bedroom space. I shared a bedroom with Sue – just the two of us in one room – how cool was that! One night we were talking before dozing off to sleep and for some reason dad come upstairs and sat on the floor along the 'landing' area. The landing light was on and as our bedroom door was open, I was able to enjoy the light that shone through. We began to whisper quietly so as not to upset dad. Suddenly, Sue was staring at me with very fixed eyes. I asked her what was wrong and she very calmly said "there's a big spider climbing up the side of your bed". I slowly moved forward to look on the edge of my bed and there it was, a monster of a spider crawling closer to my pillow. I screamed for dear life and scrambled to the end of my bed by which time dad had come in and turned the light on and clouted me to be quiet. There was a load of commotion and within seconds several faces appeared at the top of the stairs and mum made her way towards me, defusing the whole spider event. Dad did squash the monster of a spider (it was enormous, honest!) and then sent everyone back to where they came from; a bit like in a film - "off you go, there's nothing to see here. Everyone can go home now."

When Andy was born and mum brought him home from hospital, the atmosphere seemed a bit tense. Mark and I had been playing in the garden. At the end of the garden was a patch where dad put the ashes from the coal fire and we had gone there to play. We were pretending to be cowboys and were shooting 'Indians'. We got a good effect of the invisible bullets hitting the ground by stumping the tip of our shoes into the coal dust causing a puff of 'smoke' from the ashes which looked rather like gun shots that fell into the ground and a flurry of smoke blew in the gentle breeze. Mark could imitate the sound of shots being fired really well! It was fun until we got inside the house and dad was furious that we had trodden in ash type foot prints into the house! We sorted ourselves out but we really wanted to go out for a second round of shooting. As the Health Visitor had arrived this was excellent timing to sneak out into the garden and continue our play time. Then we heard dad's booming voice 'what are you doing?'.
I trembled with fear and instantly knew we were in deep trouble because we had knowingly been disobedient by getting our shoes dirty again. We got inside and we were sent to our rooms but I could hear the Health Visitor trying to 'play' things down by saying something along the lines 'they are just children playing!' My fear was, what was going to be our punishment for our disobedience because there were always

consequences for our actions. (I think we were probably smacked on the legs – which was allowed in those days).

I had recurring dreams which I kept to myself, I didn't think dreams meant anything anyway, but the Snake one I hated! I dreamt that there were loads of snakes crawling at the end of my bed and wrapping themselves around my legs – they were colourful but I started to go to bed all curled up in a ball so that my feet weren't available for the snakes to coil round at the end of my bed.

The other dream (which *did* become more significant in later years) was that the doctor from my favourite children's programme Belle et Sebastian – Dr Guillaume - found me unconscious, I don't know where, but he picked me up and carried me to safety. But then I would wake up in my dream in an English hospital with only my tummy going up and down allowing me to breath and people poking me!! No one could work out what the problem was. That was just weird. But what was comforting is that Dr Guillaume came to find me and took me to that place of safety. It wasn't a scary dream because there was excitement that all would be sorted out and I just knew I wasn't on my own. Still strange though and it came so close to being true. Maybe it was a warning from God? God has the Bigger Picture; He knows what's ahead. If my earthly dad knew there was a problem ahead, he would warn me, because he loves me. But at the time I didn't see this as a warning, just a dream. Was Dr Guillaume really Jesus because I couldn't actually see his face.

6 House Keeping

As soon as you were seven years old you were added to the rota. If you ever said that you were bored mum would soon find you something to do!

Mum made a rota (Fig. 1) that was in the kitchen to help with duties around the house. The jobs circulated each week (Eunice's idea) for Washing Up, Wiping Up, Clean Dining Room, Get Bread, Washing and Stairs, Clear Table, Lay Table and Airing. (This chart is from Ruth's school project in 1967).

To be changed once a week.	ASH UP	WIPE UP	CLEAN SITTING ROOM	CLEAN DINNING ROOM	GET BREAD WASHING STAIRS	CLEAR TABLE	LAY TABLE and AIRING
Sunday	UTH	TIMOTHY	DAVID	STEPHEN	PAUL	EUNICE	ANN
Monday	AUL	STEPHEN	TIMOTHY	ANN	DAVID	RUTH	EUNICE
Tuesday	IMOTHY	ANN	STEPHEN	EUNICE	RUTH	DAVID	PAUL
Wednesday	NICE	DAVID	ANN	RUTH	TIMOTHY	PAUL	STEPHEN
Thursday	DAVID	EUNICE	PAUL	TIMOTHY	ANN	STEPHEN	RUTH
Friday	PHEN	PAUL	RUTH	DAVID	EUNICE	ANN	TIMOTHY
Saturday	ANN	RUTH	EUNICE	PAUL	STEPHEN	TIMOTHY	DAVID

Fig. 1

While there were babies, there were nappies – terry toweling nappies, which were soaked in Napisan. These were in buckets and the smell was very potent so you would not want to peep under the lid at the same time you lifted the cover!

The washing was sorted into white articles, coloured and clothes with stains on. It *was* like having a Chinese Laundry with six loads that took two hours. When it was summer the whole length of the garden had a washing line *and* another line across the bottom of the garden where everything was hung up to dry. Mum later had a rotary dryer for all the smaller things like socks and little t-shirts etc.

To help with the washing, which seemed an enormous task, you had to be tall and strong ones! I was short and I would normally get wet sleeves, even standing on a stool. We had a 'twin tub' which was very efficient in cleaning everything. The sheets would come out brilliant white. The water would be very hot and we used these big wooden tongs to push the clothes down into the water before programming the machine to wash. Once the items had gone through the cycle you had to pull the mangled, tangled clothes out of the washing tub side into the spinner. This meant we had to squeeze as much water out of the clothes, towels or sheets and squeeze the washed articles into the spinner tub. It was long-winded but as I said before, very efficient. If the twin tub was out of order or there was too much washing it was a visit to the launderette for someone.

I remember Sue and I walking to the launderette at 'Noad's Corner'. We were probably about 7 or 8 and we had a push chair or a shopping trolley with wheels full of Saturday's washing. By the time we were old enough to do this there were less of us at home and it would usually be the big things like sheets. Mum came with us to begin with to teach us how to use the machines and then when we were confident, we did the trip on our own. Once we had put the washing in, we would cross the road to the sweet shop and would spend all our 'pocket money' on sweets. We would stuff ourselves with the yummiest sweet treats which really didn't last very long so, we chatted mostly while we waited for the washing cycle to finish. Then it was another wait before the tumble dryer finished. We managed to fold the sheets and shirts etc. between us and place all the clean clothes back into the bags and wheel them all the way back home. It was about 15 or 20 minutes' walk home. There were regular visitors to the launderette that we got to know (but can't remember their names). An older couple would be there who had two poodles. They were white, or should I say whitish, with gunk around their eyes. Although the poodles' fur was soft and curly, they weren't very cuddly.

On other Saturdays, as well as the washing, Sue and I would go shopping for Mum. There were two main shops on the way to the launderette, one was the Co-operative and the other was the International Store (which was next door to the bakers at Noad's Corner). Sometimes we were allowed to buy a Lardy Cake from Noad's bakery – a bit like a huge sugary Chelsea bun. If you have never had one it's dough cake, bread with sugar on top and fruit in it. Mum would write out a shopping list with some things to buy at the Co-op' and other items to buy at the International Store depending who had the cheapest product on the list. Mum was very good at keeping a record of the cheapest prices.

Then Saturday afternoon was usually spent doing some hobby (later years – homework) or watching a 'western' or wrestling on the television with Dad in the lounge. Dad loved watching the wrestling. He would be on the edge of his seat and shouting out "Go on! Go on!" And Mum used to say, "Dear, don't get so excited." But that didn't stop him. He was practically there!

In those days, when you went to school (junior school) on Monday morning, you had to get your diary book out and write about your weekend. My problem was that it was the same every week "I went to the launderette with my sister, Sue. We got sweets from the shop and did the shopping for Mum as well. On Sunday, we went to church and Sunday School in the afternoon and church in the evening." I wonder what my teacher thought about us going to the launderette every week when we were so young? I chuckle about it now to myself and I'm sure we all look back as a family and think about what we had to do. To us it was normal though and if you think about it, we had good domestic skills at a young age – even the boys! It was some years later before Mum and Dad were able to invest in a 'proper' washing machine. Mum didn't know herself when they bought one as she had extra time to do things rather than watch over the washing.

The shopping list, when we were all at home included:

<u>The Bread</u>
<u>Through the Week</u>
<u>on an Average</u>

Monday	2 Loaves
Tuesday	3 Loaves (delivered with the Groceries)
Wednesday	2 Loaves
Thursday	2 Loaves
Friday	2 Loaves
Saturday Sunday	5 Loaves and 1 Hovis (brown) Loaf.

The number of loaves a day differ quite a bit depending on what everyones appitite is like.

The cost of bread is about 25/- per. week.

THE MILK THROUGH THE DAY

(with 8pts. per week day)

After breakfast is finished

9.15 a.m. there are 7¼pts.

10.00 a.m. there are 6½pts.

12.15 a.m. there are 5½pts.

4.00 p.m. there are 4pts.

5.30 p.m. there are 3½pts.

8.45 p.m. there are 1½pts.

A Typical Weekly Grocery Order

		s.	d.
3 doz.	Standard eggs	11	0
½ lb.	Back Bacon	3	0
1½ lb.	Mild cheese	4	10
1 lb.	Spar butter	3	2
10lb.	Sugar	7	6
7 lb.	Spar Margarine	9	4
1 lb.	Premium Tea	6	4
2 pkts.	Giant Cornflakes	4	11
2 lge.	Weetabix	5	4
1	Spar cheese spread		10½
1 lb.	Sausages	2	9
2 pkts.	Spar crisps	1	11
6 pkts.	Spar Biscuits	4	6
2 pkts.	Gypsy Cream biscuits	2	4
1 pkts.	Spar Choc. Biscuits	1	4
2 lb.	Bananas	3	2
1 lb.	Eating Apples	1	11
1 tin	Corned Beef	4	4½
2 lge.	Fish Fingers	5	0
1 sm.	Cod Fillets	2	3
1 lb.	Spar Strawberry Jam	1	11
1 lb.	Spar Blackcurrant Jam	1	11
1 lb.	Spar Lemon Curd	2	0
1 lb.	Lime marmalade	1	5
5 tins	Kit-e-Kat	3	6½
2 tins	Princes Salmon	3	0
2	Shippams Paste	2	8
15lbs.	Potatoes	6	3
2 tins	Garden peas	3	0
1 box	Greens Sponge Mixture	1	1
2 tins	Heinz Baked Beans	3	2
2 lge.	Pork Luncheon Meat	6	6
1 tin	Beetroot		11½
1 tin	Marvel Milk	2	3
1	Bottle Spar Orange Juice	2	0
1 tin	Evaporated Milk	1	3
1 pint	Milk		10
1 tin	Sardines	1	3
4	Sliced Loaves	5	10
3 lb.	Flour	1	9
1	Giant Omo	3	2
1	Spar washing up liquid	1	11
1	Scott Kitchen Roll	1	9
1	Golden Babe Nappies	1	9
2	Bath Size toilet soap	3	0
1	Flat toilet paper	1	3
1	Reel White Sylko		9
1	comb		9
1	writing Pad	1	0
1 pkt.	Envelopes		6
	£7	16	9

This order does not include the week's bread, fish and fresh meat.

On average we would have 17 loaves of bread a week and 8 pints of milk a day. The milkman would deliver a crate of milk a day. (These lists Ruth had in her School Project about her family life in 1967).

7 Strawberries, Salisbury and the Dead Sparrow

One day, before I started school the doorbell rang. It was 'Aunty Dot'. She wasn't a real Aunt but she lived down the road from us and I understood her to be one of Mum's friends. There she was at the door, talking to Mum, having a laugh about this and that and discussing the price of bread. They were funny to listen to – I didn't have a clue what they were saying really, but Mum used to talk much broader when Aunty Dot came round. Very, very West Country or Wiltshire type accent. She handed Mum a punnet of strawberries which Mum handed to me and asked me to put in the kitchen. For some reason, I sat on the bottom step of the stairs and waited. I waited some more and more but these ladies were 'talking for England'. Well, I was enjoying the smell of the strawberries and thinking that Mum wouldn't notice if just one was missing, so I popped one into my mouth and before I knew it, I had eaten more than half of the container! And, oh dear, I began to feel sick. At this point Mum and Aunty Dot were completing their meeting of setting the world to rights and Mum's face, as she closed the door, was a picture of just, being aghast! From that day on I have never really liked strawberries. If they are placed in front of me then I will try and eat them but please, no sympathy – it was my own fault!

Next to us was the doctor's surgery, which was at the end of a row of shops with a lay-by. There was a DIY shop called Russell's, then a door which took you upstairs to the Barber's (I think he was called Michael), a grocery shop which then was run by Mr and Mrs Diaper – the shop was known as "The Diapers"! – and a hairdresser's called Ruby's and a bus stop. Then about 5 or 6 houses further away was an old lady called Mrs Salisbury. The only thing was I couldn't say Salisbury. To me she was Mrs Strawberry for quite some time. Mum would visit her on a regular basis and I remember Mark and I (probably Sue at times) visiting this old, terraced, house with an old 'Strawberry lady'. The best thing about going along with Mum to her house was not the cup of tea but her special tin. In her tin she had biscuits and chocolate ones and best of all, very often she had chocolate fingers – wow, what a treat! I would get very excited about this tin and would make the chocolate fingers last as long as possible by nibbling off the chocolate down one side and try and turn it round to devour the other side. A bit difficult most times because the chocolate was melting in my fingers and slipping out of my hand but still very yummy. I'm not sure if my Mum ever worked out why I was so keen to go with her to visit Mrs Salisbury.

Walking home from junior school one day, I walked across the big playing field where there was a tidy row of conker trees along the walled edge of the school grounds. To exit the grounds there were some large green metal gates where you were greeted by the 'lollypop man'. He was usually a happy chap and would often give you a greeting of some kind that would make you smile. Once across the road I noticed a little sparrow in the gutter upside down with its feet in the air. It was sad to see him/her there and my heart cried to see it all alone with the cars and lorries thundering past. So, I picked up the little bird, cradled it in my cupped hands and took it home to bury it.

Mum was in the garden and I called out to her "Mum, look what I've found!". To her horror she saw the dead bird in my hands and said "Why on earth did you bring that home?" She couldn't believe it and wanted me to get rid of it quickly in case it was riddled with fleas. But I said it was cute and sad and I just wanted to bury it. She came round to the idea and helped me wrap the bird in tissues and dug a little hole in the ground and we laid him/her to rest.

8 School

When I started school, I didn't understand why I couldn't stay at home, where it was warm, comfortable, and I could do what I wanted. Why did I have to leave Mum? They asked me silly questions about how many ducks were on the card. (The 'number cards' were stuck on the wall). This was apparently what they called counting. Well, I just thought this was a very confusing game!! It took me quite a while to get the hang of those ducks because I'm sure one or two kept disappearing. Then we had to find the card with our name on it – but I hadn't actually seen the whole of my name written down, so I grabbed something that looked like Christine and started to copy the letters on a sheet of paper until the teacher stopped me and said "that's not your name that's Catherine". Oh well, it was close!

By the time I was six I was in Mrs Axford's class. To me, she was big and round with a very, very loud voice. She would shout at pupils which I found very scary and I was quite frightened of her so I devised a plan! I had headaches quite often and I managed to make a headache and earache stretch out for two weeks - the most painful bit of staying home was my brother Mark saying I was making it all up and teasing me for not really being ill; I had been found out. When Mum thought I had been home long enough Mum walked me to school the following Monday morning. I just hoped that maybe Mrs Axford's behaviour had improved since I last saw her – she needed 'time out' too. We got to the classroom door and I got cold feet and held onto the door post with all my strength. Mum couldn't understand it and why she had to wrestle with me at the door. The next minute Mum had dragged me into the cloak-room and was speaking to Mrs Axford. I, very, very reluctantly changed my shoes into my 'daps' scowling as I pulled them over my feet. Then Mum and Mrs Axford came over and had a 'little chat' with me and asked what the problem was. I eventually gave some clues and I think they both seemed relieved that there wasn't any bullying or something like that. Mrs Axford said 'I only shout at the naughty boys and girls and you are very quiet so I'm not getting cross with you. You've got nothing to worry about'. So back to school it was. Mrs Axford's conduct didn't improve and I think I should have put her in detention because she continued to shout with that all booming, wrathful voice.

I hated reading – I just couldn't understand or see how the letters made the words. It wasn't until I was about 13 and in my second year at secondary school that I began to read with more ease even if I did stumble over every other word. So, I was slow at school and very average really. Art was my favourite subject and I wanted to become an artist when I left school. But then I also wanted to be a gymnast, maybe a nurse, nursery nurse or work with animals. Sadly, I didn't do any of these. I hated math's but ended up with a job with numbers!!?? It's strange what life throws at you.

The biggest fun at junior school was the autumn leaves that fell from the row of conker trees. They would fall in a multitude when it was windy on those gusty autumn days but with such elegance and grace when there was a gentle breeze. The colours were beautiful and when they were crisp and dry you could charge through them to make that crispy, crunchy noise under your shoes or throw them in handfuls to rain down over yourself and others.

Also, around September or October when the conkers would ripen and fall to the ground you could collect the shiny conkers. The green, prickly outer casings would split and burst open revealing the glossy, brown seeds inside. We collected many of these conkers and in those days, you could play 'conkers.' You would get a skewer and push it through from the top, all the way down the middle and thread a small length of string, make a knot and then you were ready to play conkers by aiming to hit your opponent's conker on their string. If theirs split – you won! Great fun if you kept winning but mind your fingers or knuckles. So, my question is, how did my brother Mark, win so many times? What did he polish it with I wonder? Sadly, conkers are like flowers. They begin to lose their fresh look by drying up, fading, and shriveling. Those shiny outer coats would appear dull and the fun appeal was gone.

Secondary school was *not* fun. We had homework, lots of it, and because I was slow at everything, I would be still doing my homework at 1 o'clock in the morning. But as time went on, I thought 'I can't keep up with this' so, I would write or do my math's until 9pm and then call it a day. Whatever was not finished was just NOT finished because I was too tired to get up in the morning if I stayed up later.

I had a couple of friends but I was mostly a loner because other girls thought I was different – probably from the way I dressed or just because I was shy and quiet? My school uniform was second hand or hand-me-downs. Things did change a bit when we all had to talk about something, anything we wanted but it had to be for two minutes. But it was up at the front of the class and our English teacher, Mrs Hall, recorded it on a tape recorder as well. I am not sure what the purpose of the exercise was but it could have been something to do with giving us confidence to stand up and give a speech with a microphone in one hand? However, when it was my turn during the whole two minutes, no one said a word, you could hear a pin drop and mouths were wide open and jaws touched the desks (not really but it does sound dramatic don't you think!?).

All I talked about was my family. How many there were of us, our names, ages and what each one did. My English teacher could not believe it and was clearly impressed. The girls in my class must have felt sorry for me as some of them very kindly brought me presents of chocolate, pencils and such because, maybe, they thought I wouldn't get anything. They were nearly right. We were allowed 50p until inflation rose or when we were older. If you were eighteen or twenty-one *then* you had a special present. I had a lovely alarm clock for my eighteenth – I loved that clock!

9 The Bunk Beds

Sue and I had bunk beds at one point. They may not have been the same bunk beds that Steve and Tim had, I'm not sure.

I slept on the top and Sue on the lower deck. One night I was stretching down, over to Sue trying to scare her or something silly and what happened? Yes, you've guessed it - I fell off it. Dad and Mum came rushing in - Dad was angry and said 'you shouldn't have been messing around' and I naughtily replied 'I just wanted the loo'. What a fibber! But I thought that if I gave a reasonable answer Dad wouldn't get angry and I wouldn't be at the end of his wrath. As it was, I did need the toilet and there was blood dripping out of a cut at the back of my ankle. Ouch! It looked deep, but just a plaster would fix it, so, Mum patched me up and I was put back to bed. That put an end to us messing around at night time.

If we were playing 'hide and seek' the bottom deck of the bunk bed was a brilliant place to hide. All you had to do was put a blanket over yourself in the corner or curl up on the top bed and nestle by the wall. Anyone rushing into the bedroom looking for you wouldn't see you if they just fleeted in and out of the room. But then it became a favourite hiding place and didn't seem to be such an ingenious idea after all.

Another incident while we had the bunks was when Mark, Sue and I were sitting on the top bunk where you could touch the ceiling. We decided to check out the polystyrene tiles on the ceiling. They felt funny to touch. We looked at them slowly and dug our finger nails in a couple of times only to discover that they were made up of these little tiny balls of white foam beads and if you scratched them a bit, we realised we could make some snow by scratching the tiles. This was great fun, very realistic and effective. It was the summer holidays if I remember rightly, Mum eventually came up to our room to see what we were having fun with. Her face looked horrified, her jaw dropped and a worried look that said it all "what am I going to tell your dad when he gets home?". I don't really remember Dad getting very cross about this event, though; maybe he thought it was funny? Or maybe Mum said something to him which smoothed things over.

10 Visitors

It wasn't very often we had visitors but when we did there was great excitement, for us anyway. Mum and dad seemed to know quite a few people; I think mainly from church. We would have visiting speakers for tea before the evening service. That meant a 'posh' tea! Cake *and* trifle!

One of these special visitors travelled a lot and usually visited us on his way home, often from places we had never heard of and whose names we could not pronounce. He was an honorary uncle, not a "real" uncle – but Uncle Frank was special, because of who and what he was but especially because of how he made us feel. When Uncle Frank died in 1989, his son said that he was one of the bravest men he had ever met. As children we just knew he was special.

In 1971 the Missionary Society of which he was the Honorary Chairman began a new magazine which today is called Frontlines. Uncle Frank had a way with words, a way of telling a sto- ry which got you hooked and made you laugh, and yet without in any way hiding the very real challenges and dangers that were often part of the story. But perhaps the greatest chal- lenge he ever faced personally was in his final years when Parkinson's Disease took away his ability to speak – but not his ability to think and take in what was happening around him. His smile will always stick with me.

One of our visitors told a joke but I can't remember if it was Uncle Frank or not but it made everyone laugh. It was about a young girl:

Her Daddy asked her what she would like for her birthday. She said she would really like some perfume and a watch, because she would feel grown up, like Mummy. So, on her birthday she was very excited about the whole day and even her favourite Uncle was coming to tea. She sat proudly next to her uncle at tea time and would give a wriggle now and then hoping he would notice her perfume or at least hear her new watch ticking. It was time for her uncle to leave and she was slightly upset that he hadn't made any comment about her per- fume or new watch. She kissed her uncle goodbye and proudly said "if you heard a little noise and smelt a little smell, it was me"!!!!

When Eunice left home and came back to visit, I thought I would burst with excitement! She brought laughter and happiness with her. She was my fun sister who made things happen in what seemed a world of impossibilities to me. She was ambitious and at a young age knew she wanted to be a missionary. She has been a very dedicated and committed missionary for over forty years!

We had other speakers, pastors and friends for tea and I loved how mum managed to produce lovely food on those days.

11 Holidays

Uncle Frank and his wife Lillian ran a Christian Guest House in Weston-Super-Mare called Berachah (which means Blessing).

The first holiday mum and dad had at Berachah was in 1956 with five children then. I remember going as a child but I would be travel sick every time, so the travelling wasn't fun. I would have to take travel sickness tablets which made me very, very sleepy – I must have seemed drunk! Mum and dad had friends with cars as mum never learnt to drive and dad wasn't allowed to drive because of his black-outs. So, we travelled in two cars. The other way to travel to Weston-Super-Mare was by mum collecting vouchers from the packets of cornflakes or washing powder when they offered train tickets. Of course, it didn't take mum very long to collect these vouchers because we ate cornflakes by the ton and she must have gone through dozens of boxes of washing powder for all our laundry!

On arrival, just walking up the fake paving stones was a delight in itself. After ringing the bell someone would eventually answer the door and the welcome was so warming you could just melt in the hallway. Even the smell of the guest house was an aromatic reception. After a chat between mum, dad and Aunty Lillian and Uncle Frank (if he wasn't away), which seemed like a whole day to me but probably ten minutes to them, Christine, one of their daughters, would show us to our rooms. It was so exciting you could explode! The beds smelt so clean and fresh (not that ours weren't clean at home) and there was so much space! The youngest of the family which included Mark, me, Sue and Andy would be in the family room. At the top of the bedroom door there was a small glass window with coloured glass – it looked so pretty especially when the landing light was on and the glass shone with different colours. I had never seen coloured glass before.

Even looking out the main window it had a border of coloured glass panels around it! Everywhere was carpeted and there was no washing up, clearing the tables or laying the tables for us, no cooking or planning meals for mum, just Andy's baby bottles and nappies to worry about, but Aunty Lillian was really helpful. They had two daughters and a son – all lovely people and a cook but I can't remember her name. At meal times we took up two tables and most of the guests couldn't believe that we were all one family and it was often quite amusing to hear the comments made about us and it caused a lot of laughs.

We itched to go out and spy the land but we were too young to go on such adventures of curiosity by ourselves and besides mum and dad knew their way around very vividly. There was the Marine Lake, which had very muddy sea water but the sand was great. When the sea was out it went out a long distance away from land which meant you could spend hours on the main beach by the Grand Pier. Anchor Head had impressive rocks we could climb and have adventures and there was a small causeway that used to be used to take boats out. There was another pier – Birnbeck Pier. There was a ferry (I think it was a paddle steamer) that would sail from the end of this pier to Lundy Island if you could afford it.

We would take walks along the Kewstoke Road to Kewstoke where there was a lovely café. Mum and dad must have saved up a lot to be able to afford the holiday and the cups of tea we had at the café.

If we had saved our pocket money up before the holiday, we could walk down to the corner shop and buy anything within our budget. It was just exciting to go into the shop and see different things from 'Diapers' grocery shop back home. It was one of the highlights anyway. You could walk the other way, up the steep road from the guest house, to some well looked after gardens where there was a boating-pond, hidden in a corner behind a cluster of hedges. We took a wooden model boat with a sail on it and pushed it away on one side and one of us would catch it the other side but it was bad news if there wasn't any wind that day. Once we visited the pond and Sue leaned too far forward and fell in – she was soaked, head to toe. Both Mum and I walked back to the guest house with Sue and all I could hear was Sue snuffling from the shock and being so upset, but also the squelch, squelch, squelch with every step she made. That event was not fun for Sue and we all were pretty silent, feeling sorry for her.

It was a Christian Guest House, as I have already mentioned, and in the evenings, the guests would be invited to a meeting. All the adults and older members of the family would, somehow, all fit into the lounge. It was a large lounge but there were a lot of guests. There was singing and praying and someone, maybe, Uncle Frank at times, would share something from the Bible or a lesson we could learn from God's Word. As we were very young, we went to bed before the meeting. I remember once that dad had forgotten to bring the calendar with him and so he asked if any of us had a favourite Bible verse. I literally blurted out ***John Chapter 14***. I have no idea why but actually it's a well-known chapter and it is very special to me. It starts off: -

"Let not your heart be troubled: ye believe in God, believe also in me.[2] *In my Father's house are many mansions: if it were not so, I would have told you"*

Since my growing up years seemed to give me a troubled heart, I would always speak this verse in my mind and take comfort from it.

Always, on the last evening of the holiday we would go to Anchor Head and have an ice-cream and sit on the rocks. This was a real treat for us but it was also a little sad as we knew we would be going home tomorrow. I'm sure, even the seagulls were sad for us. But the sound of the waves splashing on the rocks was a beautiful sound and something to remember on our departure.

12 Being a Teenager

Growing up as a teenager – well – I wouldn't want to go through that again! I longed to be loved and to belong. But felt I didn't have either so felt quite lost. I'm sure I was the typical moody teenager and life seemed very boring, nothing happened in my life to make it exciting or different. I was not sure where I was going or what my aim was. Sue and I were close and we did look like twins for several years and Mum (and many other people) would often call us by the wrong name. I had two pet guinea pigs, Squeakie – she was gorgeous and I adored her – she was like a close friend who listened, she would purr a lot when we were having a cuddle. She had a couple of litters as the other guinea pig, was called Lawrence. I loved Squeakie so much. She died when I was 18 – oh, did I ever cry my eyes out! It sounds silly for a young adult to be upset over a guinea-pig but she was very important to me.

I have memories of kneeling down by my bed, praying and hugging my pillow, desperate for 'someone'. It seems pathetic now but at the time this was my emotional state. My heart would literally feel pained, broken and I was in agony – I never want to experience those dark days ever again but I am so thankful that I did talk to Jesus believing He would listen and understand how I was feeling. This is probably normal for a teenager, I don't know. If I hadn't talked to Jesus and believed He was listening then I would have felt more alone and very stupid. Nothing seemed to change in my situation but I didn't lose faith. Jesus helped me through those tough times I have no doubt about that. Sometimes I would cry myself to sleep because I felt so sad, unloved, I felt really sorry for myself and even though I know Mum and Dad loved me, it just seemed from a distance and not enough for me. I felt trapped, I couldn't do what I wanted or learn to be myself. In the morning my eyes would be very red and puffy and I would have a bad headache. I didn't really want to talk to anyone else about these feelings in case I was labelled as weird and wallowing in self-pity forever and a day. I had no-one to show me how to get out of this rut. Not good memories at all. Looking back, maybe it was a mix up of hormones, who knows.

Going to church was a big part of our lives as Mum and Dad were Christians so from Sunday School to Youth Groups my own interest and commitment to being a Christian began. I had to find Him myself. I felt I could pray or I asked for help if I had a problem with my school work especially mathematics and I would imagine Jesus next to me and explaining what the formula was to find the correct answer. Unfortunately, I thought that Jesus couldn't do mathematics either as I would get the answers wrong or maybe I didn't hear Him. But in secondary school I did think about God nearly all the time and I talked to Him so much because He was my friend. Even in a big family you can still feel lonely!

I pulled a daisy to pieces once (sorry daisy) but as I pulled each petal off, I was amazed how it was made. No man could make a flower or blade of grass and certainly no 'big bang' could! Am I the only person thinking this way? I have never known what it is to *not* know about God in my up-bringing. But my question is why is life so difficult? If God is a God of love, why is there crime? Why is there hate? And why are we here? Why, why, why?

'Why' is the question and everyone has to decide and make their own choices. People look at the evidence put before them and then make a judgement on what they see. I see that God made this world and He loved it. He gave man the freedom of choice. Adam had the choice whether to eat the fruit from Eve or not. I have the choice to eat cake or not. To me, cake *looks* really good and so I would choose cake. Adam, clearly loved the look of the apple and what it could do for him if he ate it, and so he chose to eat it. But sometimes there are consequences to our decisions. The cake has calories and calories don't like me! Adam ate the fruit but he then knew more about his surrounds, he knew fear and nakedness. He was frightened at his choice because God warned him not to eat it. He probably felt more than just a naughty school boy. So, he hid. If you hide, you know you have done something wrong. From then on, people did do wrong because they haven't made the right choice and things/life gets messed up. So, it's not God's fault that the world is in a mess. I can't blame God for my bad choices.

But having a relationship with someone I couldn't see was a bit more beyond my understanding really. I knew there was a creator and I knew He loved me and He died for me. But I had to find out why. One thing I did learn is that the more you talked to Him the closer you got to Him.

So, to conclude:

God is our creator – it's written in ***Genesis chapter 1 v 1*** (New International Version) *"In the beginning God created the heavens and the earth".* So, we are accountable to Him.

Man rebelled against God - ***Romans chapter 3 v 23*** (New International Version) "[23] for all have sinned and fall short of the glory of God," Death is the penalty for sin but we can't do anything to reverse this.

Jesus – God sent Jesus, His son to die on the cross for us, each one of us, and paid for our sins, defeating death.

2 Corinthians Chapter 5 v 21 (New International Version) *" [21]God made him who had no sin to be sin for us, so that in him we might become the righteousness of God."*

Response – By repenting, or turning from sin and to Jesus and placing our faith in Christ, we are saved. ***Mark Chapter 1 v15*** (New International Version) *" [15] "The time has come," he said. "The kingdom of God has come near. Repent and believe the good news!"*

Sue and I used to walk to school down the long hill (the Wellsway) and back. School was about three miles away but if you walked fast enough or did a bit of jogging you could get to school in about 45 minutes. Coming home did take a bit longer because it was up hill all the way! There was a truck of workmen who passed us at the same time every day and they would hoot their horn, and eventually we would look out for them and wave. If we did wait for a bus, it would be late or very full, then either the bus would drive right past you or it would pick you up but you had to stand all the way home.

Once a gentleman stopped to offer us a lift to school in something like an old Citroen DS (1955-1975). He said "Would you like a lift? It's ok, I know your Mum". I, very sensibly, said "No thank you" but then Sue said "Yes please". I pulled at Sue's sleeve and said "we don't know him" but Sue was insistent that we would be ok because he knew Mum. Sue was getting in the back of the car and I thought she was crazy-mad or just desperate for a lift, and me? Well, I was terrified but couldn't let Sue be kidnapped on her own so I got in with her. Shaking and panicking nearly all the way to school we did arrive and the man 'released' us without any ransom deal, outside our school *and* nobody knew anything about us being taken captive! I was cross with Sue and said we could have really been taken. I couldn't understand why she was so calm and collected about the whole event. When we got home, later that day, I told Mum what had happened and she calmly said "Oh, that's Mr O'Keefe. Yes, he's a very kind man". Eh!? Had I missed something? Did everyone in the family know this man and why didn't I know who he was? Never mind, it was all over and we were both safe. But I still wouldn't get in a stranger's car.

Sue and I often made cakes and the most enjoyable part of that was licking the bowl especially the icing one! Once we were baking but Sue thought we were making little cupcakes and I thought we were making scones so the 'cakes' came out a bit wrong – cup-scones? Scone-cakes? Wonky-cakes? Or maybe we could just call them a mess!

By now several members of the family had got married and there was only Steve, Tim, Mark, myself, Sue and Andy left at home. Paul and Dave had left home and, after university, and settled in their different jobs, they *both* married Chris's! I was Chris mark I. Pauls' Chris was mark II and they got married in 1974. Dave's Chris was mark III and they also married in 1974. Ruth married Will (William) in 1975, Eunice, left home at 17 and Ann left home to do nursing at Wellwyn Garden City, 1976.

When I was 12 and Sue was 10, we went to stay with Dave and Chris in Stoke-on-Trent. We had experiences we had never had before! We went camping in Wales for a couple of days in Rhyl, North Wales and we went to the cinema for the first time ever! We saw Cinderella and we watched our first scary film late one night – "Them!" which was made in 1954 about large ants. We were scared but now it's just an old black and white movie! We learnt a lot from Dave and Chris and I certainly realised that the world outside 492 was a great deal bigger than I ever imagined.

Going back home after such a holiday was difficult. The atmosphere was so often tense because of dad. Poor dad, I really wonder what was going through his mind in those days. You only had to spill milk in the kitchen or something and he would be really annoyed and shout at you and you would end up standing in the kitchen trembling. Everything was just too much for dad, I think. The maintenance of the house, the gardening, the finances, the mouths to feed and clothes to buy, even though there were only six of us at home now. They say it's cheaper by the dozen don't they! Somehow or other and in ways different to each other we all survived.

Most of us had hobbies, which kept us out of mischief and it was good to learn something we were good at. Steve played his guitar and he could play the piano too; Tim would make things out of wood or make chess sets out of Resin; Mark made model planes and learnt to play the violin; Sue loved reading and we both did sewing and learnt to use Mum's sewing machine which was a Singer. I learnt to sew at Junior school and one Christmas I got a book on making felt toys. I made a horse and a mouse. I went on to make other things like, the patchwork cushions, small quilts and even the Wombles! I also learnt to play the guitar but not as well as Steve could! And Andy played the piano from the age of six.

When Ruth and Will were first married, they lived in a bungalow on the Wellsway and on Mondays, after school, Sue and I would go to Red Cross 'Club'. We walked to Ruth and Will's and we had tea. I remember having Golden Syrup sandwiches and watching Hong Kong Phooey! And then we would walk onto the Red Cross group at 6.00pm.

When I was 16, I wanted to finish school and go to College in Clifton, Bristol to become a Nursery Nurse. But mum and dad said that I couldn't and that I had to go and find a job to bring some money into the home. Eunice tried to stick up for me to let me go to college, but it was not to be. It then came to me that when people ask you when you are younger what would you like to be when you're older, you can't choose after all! What a let-down!! Well, I nearly got a job at the Mineral Hospital in Bath. They were complimentary of me after the interview and asked me back for a chat even though they had offered the position to someone else. They suggested that I did more studying and then I could probably apply for a different job with them again. So mum, dad and I compromised. I went to sixth form for just one year - a Business Studies Course. Sadly, I hated it and didn't do very well. Typing (which I loved), English for Office Skills, Shorthand, Commerce and Accounts. It was the longest year ever! I got the certificates for all except Shorthand because I think I made up my own style of Shorthand that nobody could understand – what you don't know, you make up!

I learnt that even your parents, inadvertently, can let you down but there are no perfect parents around actually, it's a fact. But they were doing the best they could. The thing is, that children don't come with a manual. In a big family you learnt to accept situations for what they were. You would often find that you have that thought "well, that's the way things are. Accept and it and move on."

In 1978, I was 15 or 16 at the time, I got baptised with my sister and brother as well as 3 others in our youth group at Southstoke Evangelical Free Church. I was in such a hurry to be baptised I slipped up much to my embarrassment! But it was a good day and it was because I love Jesus that I wanted to do this.

When Mark, Sue, I and Andy were in our teens' we went to Widcombe Baptist Church in Bath. We often felt 'out of it' mainly because we were 'working class' and most of the people there were 'middle class'. It's a shame that there are any 'classes' at all in churches. But I still liked the people and we got on with a large number of them, they were just in a different class of society to us.

Mark bought a Single Lens Reflex camera (SLR) and he taught me how to use it. This was a great opening to life in Widcombe because a number of the youth group had SLR's and it meant that we had something in common. It was such a bonus because I loved this new found hobby.

The Pastor, then, was Peter Culver and the Assistant Pastor was John Hodder. John was the Youth Pastor and he did a good job too! There were about 60 teenagers in the youth group and some very vibrant young Christians. A lot of them came from Bath University but also a good percentage were still local. I had two cousins there – well, their mum is my second cousin. Paul, I used to call him "Cuz". It seemed very fitting for him. His sister, Sarah, was always friendly, very confident and a clever girl but I didn't speak to her a great deal but just to be near her you could pick up these 'happy vibes' because she was so bubbly.

John Hodder was married to Janet and at that time they had a young girl called Rachel. Later Philip came along and quite often Sue and I would baby-sit for them. Janet seemed to always have the sniffles and she said once that 'they' thought she was allergic to John's beard!

I had a few guitar lessons with John on a Friday afternoon around 4pm (this was not long before I left the Sixth Form). But sometimes we would take the opportunity to talk about God. I shared with him how unhappy I was at home. The only way I could explain how I felt at the time was that there was a Brick Wall in front of me and I couldn't get over it or round it and that sometimes I didn't feel that I was a Christian. He taught me not to be so 'inward looking' and not to go by my 'feelings' so much. A good lesson to learn. He encouraged me to pray at lunchtimes with a friend – Suzanna Craig. Through this I realised life isn't easy but God is a God of love and patience and He was very real.

Another young couple that I got to know were Tat and Alan and they had two young children, Matthew and Sarah, very cute children. I did some baby-sitting for them as well as for Jan and John. Tat (a nurse) has a lovely smile that brightens up the whole room when she enters it and Alan (a doctor) is softly spoken and is very caring. But I was sad to learn that they were 'called' to leave for a while to become missionaries in Kathmandu, Nepal. I was very down about this because they were lovely people and I was just getting to know them. During their time over there they extended their family and had a third child, Andrew. It was quite some time before I met Andrew as they were away for a very long time - I have no doubt they would have been brilliant missionaries out there, bless them. (They are home now and we do keep in touch).

On Sunday afternoons, when the whole house was quiet, dad would have a nap. I would go into what was my own room by then, and open the Bible and have a go at reading. I skipped over the words that I couldn't understand as it was easier to pass over them than to look them up every time; it seemed almost every other word was a difficult one. I tried reading the Bible but really couldn't understand it, it didn't really make sense. But I loved reading about Abraham, Moses, Daniel, Nehemiah, Ruth and the birth of Jesus. They made sense and good reading. As the weeks went by, I got an overall picture that this Bible was full of different books written by different people that God inspired them to put pen to paper. God gave those writers the words to write. It is His history book. If we didn't realise there was a creator that made us, sea, sky, flowers, grass etc then you had a second chance by reading His book to learn that He is the Creator.

13 Going Out To Work

I left school at nearly eighteen years old and my first job was at the University of Bath as an Accounts Clerk. This didn't seem a good choice because I was rubbish at math's! But actually, it was the best job I ever had! It took about six months to settle into the post and get used to no half terms or long seasonal holidays. The people were lovely and the work was challenging and interesting. It did get a bit boring when you learnt it so well and back to front but as long as you didn't make a boring job boring it was fine! Thankfully it was a busy office and very few quiet times. To begin with, several people in the office where I was based were seasonal/summer workers and just 5 weeks into the job, they left and there was just me and my boss, Phil Hill. Talk about being put in at the 'deep end'! Two went off to the college and the other one, Vaughn, decided to leave but, apparently, regretted it later.

Mr Ian Trickett was my main boss and although he would get stressed and lose his rag sometimes, he was a good manager. Everyone respected him and was given the title of Uncle Ian! Phil was a great boss too but he didn't become an 'uncle' because he was too young, I think. He was quite quiet, calm and a patient sort of chap.

One of the first tasks he gave me was to look up all the payments for a Mrs R Hooper for the last year. When I had done this and presented him with my findings I asked "Why do you need this information? She's my sister." With surprise he said "Ohhh, is she? Well, you are probably wondering why then. It's because she needs a new contract for her position." Although Ruth didn't and doesn't work for the University, BIME (as it was known then) was supported by the University as well as the local health board and they set up the Charity which is now known as Designability.

The challenging part of this job was all down to the details with checking all the figures, numbers, addresses, documents and correct names. I just loved it!

At Bath University there was a staff swimming pool and I became a member and used to go swimming during lunchtimes. If I could do twenty-two lengths, I was impressed with myself. This is when I thought it was important to keep fit. So, I went jogging too. Not every day though. I would jog from our house to Midford castle. It was a lovely scenic route, fields, trees, hills in the distance and beautiful flowers on the way. It was one and a half miles there so three miles altogether. How amazing it was to be able to put one foot in front of the other and get from one place to another under my own steam. I'm not sure what I was doing wrong but I could not make myself do any more than three miles. My body just wouldn't or couldn't run more, I couldn't build up to four miles even. This made me very frustrated with myself.

About this time, I would feel faint in the office and at other times had a real, deep exhausting feeling. Maybe, it was the swimming and jogging? Reluctantly, I gave up this 'keep fit' idea but it was a long time before I stopped having these episodes of feeling faint and exhausted. My colleagues were a bit concerned and told me I should talk or see someone about it. I told myself that I was imagining it and it would go away. It did eventually go away but I have never found out why I don't have the ability to train up for something like running a marathon, which was one of my life-time dreams, which I don't think I'll be doing now.

Anyway, back to jobs. I had many different jobs and gained a deal of experience. I worked for the M.O.D., a builder's construction business as an Accounts Clerk, but because I wouldn't lie for them, they asked me to leave. I was an Assistant Matron at a girls' boarding school, an Accounts Clerk for a Friendly Society, Accounts Clerk for Chartered

Accountants, Word Processing/Audio Typist at two different insurance companies: firstly, Sphere Drake who insured large ships and then, Commercial Union insurance, in the Marketing Department. Then I had three different jobs as an Accounts Assistant, then as a Credit Controller and later a Loss Adjuster for Gan Insurance in the City of London who mostly insured airplanes. So, I had quite a list of various positions in different establishments.

Reverse back to Bath University; there were two other girls who worked at the University in the Cashier's Department (Janet and Anne) and we all bought ourselves motorbikes and passed our tests on them. Around 1981, Jan and John moved away from Widcombe Baptist Church, Bath to pastor a church of their own in Snettisham, Norfolk, and I wanted to go and see them on my Yamaha V50 motorcycle. I think my colleagues thought I was a bit crazy going all that way on a 50cc bike, but I was determined to go.

It was John Hodder's Induction Service, and I set out on my bike to Snettisham; my aim was to be at the service. But alas, it took me so long to get there that I didn't get there until it was too late. I had never had to navigate before so I got a little lost and in total it took me 9 hours. I only had a map then – Sat Nav's hadn't been invented then and I ended up going the wrong way. It was getting late and I had only just got on the right road in the right direction. It wasn't my original plan. I searched for somewhere to stay overnight but couldn't find anything as I seemed to be out in the sticks. I then saw, what looked like a newly built farm house. I knocked on the door and asked them if they knew of any Bed and Breakfasts where I could stay that night. But they said they didn't really know of anywhere close by except a Pub. I wasn't keen on that idea but as we were chatting over a cup of coffee that they had kindly given me I saw a Bible on the side table. I boldly asked them if they were Christians and they said yes! Straightaway, there was a great connection and they invited me to stay the night there with them. I felt safe enough to say yes and they gave me breakfast the next morning and waved me on my way. I did get to Snettisham, just very, very late! Needless to say, it was a long weekend and I picked up the worst cold ever. But it was lovely to see Jan, John, Rachel and Philip.

A short while later I bought a slightly bigger bike! A Yamaha RS100. The model was really the size of a 125cc which meant that I could just about touch the floor when I stopped at a junction. I did try giving Mark, my brother, a lift on the back of it but he fell off a couple of times. I don't think Mark has a very good sense of balance, which he would admit to.

I did take my bike up to Snettisham again and this time I didn't go via Gloucester and it didn't take me 9 hours. I did have a slight problem with the 'new' bike on the way up to Norfolk. The chain needed tightening up and it poured with rain. I stopped at a petrol station and decided to fill up as I hadn't put any petrol in the tank since leaving Bath. It wasn't a self-service petrol station then and the old gentleman proceeded to fill the petrol tank but I didn't realise that I had hardly used any fuel and petrol spilt everywhere and all down my waterproof all-in-one outfit. He, kind of, chuckled annoyingly but didn't charge me and I left rather embarrassed and smelling of petrol! I got as far as Cambridge and then I rang John to say that I was nearly at Snettisham but the bike was playing up. It seemed to be smoking a lot. After some suggestions of what to do I decided to ride a bit longer and see how I got on. But a little further on I was so worried about the motorbike blowing up that I stopped at another telephone box and John decided to come and meet me with a flat-bed truck. He arrived and it started to rain – again! There was no way we could roll the bike up the planks of wood up onto the truck, it was too steep an angle and I don't think I was much help either. Then John said to turn the bike on and see where the smoke was coming from. I turned the engine on and we waited while the engine ticked over and warmed up again. Then, there it was! "There it is John!" I said, "Where?" John asked. "There! It's coming from the exhaust pipe!". Well, John chuckled and chuckled some more and said "Chris! That's just steam!" How stupid was I but what a huge relief! I had a good weekend with the family and I enjoyed teaching young Philip the days of the week, Tuesday was his favourite word! John tightened up the chain and Jan washed my smelly outfit. It felt like a safe, warming but busy home.

On my way home I stalled the motorbike on a steep hill. I just couldn't get it going again. I had probably 'flooded' the engine, so, I got off the bike and pushed it to a level part of the road and waited a bit until I thought the engine was 'unflooded'. Thankfully, the engine reared up and off I travelled the rest of my journey home. But little did I know that that was the last time I would see John.

I had strained my back when pushing my motorbike up the hill, and the result was lower back pain, which is an awful spot to try and comfort or massage yourself, and it was taking ages to recover from the strain. So, I decided to sell the bike and buy a car. It was a drier way to travel and it was certainly more balanced with four wheels instead of two and I didn't feel so vulnerable.

A short time after, Abigail Hodder was born; so, their family was growing and I couldn't wait for another opportunity to visit them. Sadly, John had become unwell with flu type symptoms and he just kept getting worse. The whole of Widcombe Baptist Church was praying for his recovery. We were all praying for a miracle.

One morning, I think it was a Monday, I woke up at 4am with a start. It was weird. There was no noise in the house I could hear that would have startled me in my sleep – no one going to the bathroom or anything. So, I snuggled back down into the bed sheets but all I could think of was John and Janet and Janet being lonely. Had John died? Something has happened, I could feel it deep down. Later that morning I learnt that John had passed away at 4am. Thank you, Lord, – you gave me a little bit of warning. I was still upset. Apart from Gran I hadn't really known anyone close to me who had died. It wasn't a nice feeling at all, it's a sad, empty, lost feeling.

I went to the funeral with some friends and it was hard to believe, for all of us there that day, that John was no more. Jan was very brave and coped with Rachel, Philip and Abigail so well. Abigail was only a toddler and had no idea what was going on. I couldn't get over the fact that she no longer had a dad.

It was two years later that I went up to Snettisham, Norfolk. This time for another funeral – Jan and Rachel's. This was very sad and devastating. They had both been killed in a car accident. Janet died instantly and Rachel was on a life support machine but sadly died a week or so afterwards. So, Philip and Abigail became orphans at a very young age. I remember seeing John's Mum. She was so upset but kept it together as much as she could for the children's sake.

John's Mum passed away around 2014. The children were adopted by Mr and Mrs Macauley who lived in Cambridge. Philip now lives in London and Abigail married, has three children and lives in America.

Mum and Dad married 28th August 1948 at Longmead in Bath.

Concorde rings and Dad on the right (with glasses)

Ann Eunice Ruth Dave Paul

Steve Tim Mark Chris Sue
(November 1966)

Mark and I together in the garden.

Our House – 492

Our Gran.

(From left to right – top row)
Eunice, Paul (with the glasses on), Ruth, Dave, Ann

(From left to right – bottom row)
Sue, Dad and Andy on his lap, Tim, Mark, Steve, Mum, Chris

Me and Sue.

Our garden and the cooking apple tree.

Uncle Frank
(Courtesy of his daughter Ruth Doolan)

Uncle Frank and his wife Lillian ran a Christian Guest House in Weston- Super-Mare called Berachah (which means Blessing).

Eunice and me in Phuket, Thailand – 1989

Eunice and me riding on an elephant

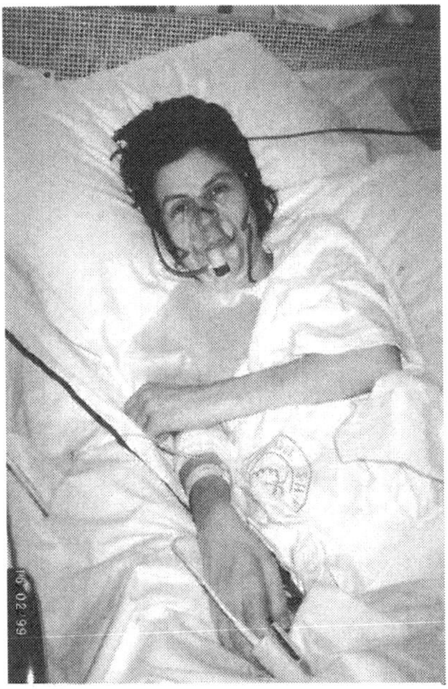

Really not feeling well – Feb 1999

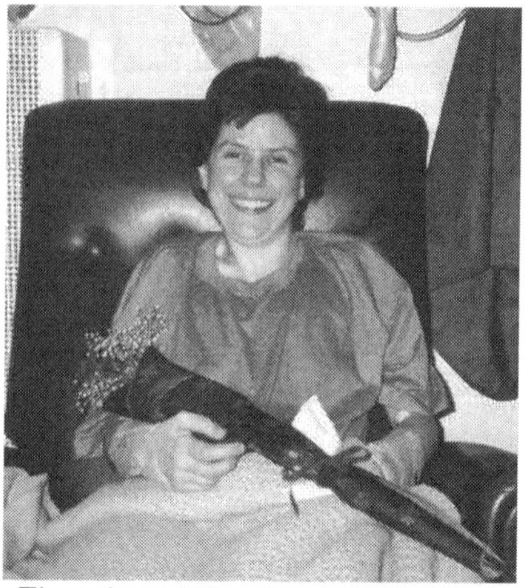
First day sitting in an arm chair

Bryony, me and Jo walking along the bars.

My first Progress Report that Eunice wrote for me:

PROGRESS REPORT from CHRIS

Dear Friends and Family,

Many thanks for your cards, flowers and well wishes; I've really appreciated them all.

As you can imagine it has been rather a shock – to be walking on Thursday morning, and then lose all feeling and movement within 6 hours. It wasn't helped by the fact that the first doctor in casualty insisted there was nothing wrong with me, and Eunice (Sister) and I spent 6-7 hours talking and crying about the situation!!! (Thank goodness Eunice was there.)

After X-rays, a CT scan, a lumber puncture and an MRI scan they finally found out what was wrong – inflammation in my upper spine (C4 and C5 for those who know about such things) then I seemed to be surrounded by doctors and 101 other people who all seemed to be official and important.

After my debut appearance on TV, they decided to move me to Frenchay, ward 2 about 2.30 on Friday afternoon. Needless to say, I was shattered and so was Eunice. Ruth, Will (Sister and Brother-in-law) and Eunice, followed me to Frenchay. By the time I arrived my lungs didn't seem to be working properly and I began to get scared. I was too "blotto" to know what they did to sort me out, but gradually it seemed to stabilise.

I was moved to ward 19 on Monday and that seems to be where I'll have to set up home for a while.

I have been able to sit up increasingly, and hope to be in a wheel chair sometime this week. My limbs are gradually responding to my brain's instructions, but still remain numb. I can feel hot and cold again, the pain in my neck and shoulder blades has been bad, and at times unbearable – I've never been so high on drugs, I don't know why people pay big money for this sensation, I don't like the side effects!!

I've been really touched and encouraged by the steady stream of visitors, I'm just sad it has to be in these circumstances. The consultant is very hopeful for a full recovery, though he is saying nothing about a time scale.

I don't know what the future may hold but I would value your prayers and support as it unfolds.

Lots of love Chris

Frenchay Hospital, Bristol

Eunice and the pink pigs

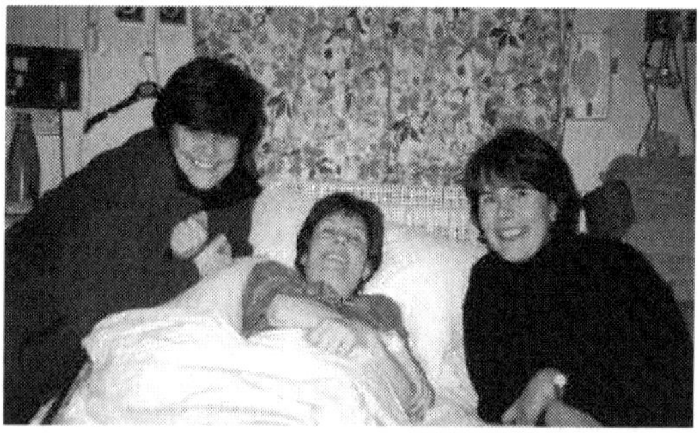

Eunice, me and Sue.

Emma, me and Alex – March 1999

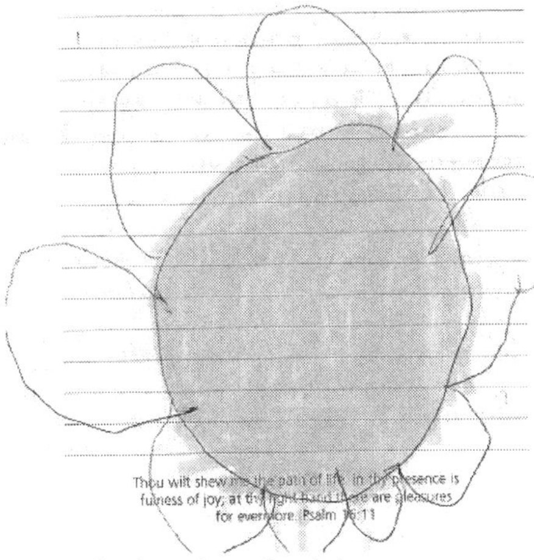

Emma's drawing of a daisy

Emma's drawing of a happy face.

My Mum and Dad

Martyn's Mum and Dad.

The 11 of us - September 2016

Steve Ann Eunice Ruth Dave Paul

Tim Mark Chris Sue Andy

Emma and Alex

Chip

This is a picture I drew on one of Jennifer Rees Larcombe's Retreat weekends 7th October 2021

Martyn, Chris, Slinky and Lilly
Summer 2022

14 Leaving Home

By the time I was twenty-two I had partly moved away from home and was working at a girls' boarding school in North Bristol. It was a good way to leave home really because I had somewhere to live during term time and went home for holidays unless I managed to stay somewhere else like Dave & Chris Ill's in Staffordshire. But it was a hard summer that year because Sue was getting married in the September and I found it so hard not to feel depressed or sad about it. Sue was my best friend and I was losing her. I wasn't jealous of her marrying Jem; I was upset that she was getting married before me; after all, I was the older one out of the two of us! I didn't even have a boyfriend so I felt lonelier than ever. Ruth was a great help and a rock to me at this time – she held my hand through the dark tunnel of loneliness. I have never forgotten what she said once; "after a storm, there's always a rainbow". It's true! She was pillar of strength, a shoulder to cry on and someone to catch my tears and pray with and for me. Ruth never judged me or criticised me. She never does about anyone. Bless her.

Sometimes, when you are so down and out of sorts you struggle to pray. It's like God has gone silent and your words are going out to no-where. But when you know others are praying for you, you do have a sense of being carried. And I think this is how I felt with Ruth's prayers.

It was an awful time to get through really; like being lost in the dark woods, going round in circles, continuously asking which way to go in my mind, just waiting and looking for the right answers or only listening to the answers that I really wanted to hear. No-one can promise anything and no-one could fully understand what I was going through. I have had friends before, looking for help and advice, a listening ear but if you didn't say exactly what they wanted to hear, they didn't want to listen – they didn't want to know. So, at one point I stood up and dusted myself down. I need to help myself and I need to face reality here. I may be single for the rest of my life or might meet someone later. The other question is, do I really need someone? Haven't I got my Heavenly Father? I do, so let me forget this problem for a moment, go away on a break and leave everything to Him.

It was the end of the summer holidays in 1985 and I decided to help out at an all-girls Christian camp near Bridgewater for the Bank Holiday weekend. This was something that Eunice introduced me to and it has always been great fun. I would go as a Tent Officer, which is a rewarding job in itself. Pam Scott-Cook (lovely, caring and kind hearted lady!) was in charge and I arrived in my red mini ready to lose myself, forget my loneliness and throw myself in to helping others. This is where I met Tim. Tim and his friend Chris Curtis (Christopher) were there to help around. Pam said we really needed some men to protect us women camping out alone in the field. And just as well they were around as there were a few problems with the lads from the farm a couple of fields away that crept over to frighten the girls as they settled down for the night. Chris happened to have his head out of the bottom of his tent, star gazing when he saw some lads sneaking towards the tents. Chris shouted 'aye!' loud enough for them to jump out of their skins and scarper back home!! Tim and I got on well and we were girl and boyfriend for about 6 or 7 years.

Later in 1989, I felt I needed to do something completely different. Eunice was home on furlough and I telephoned her to ask if I could fly back with her. But the timescale didn't really work for us to travel on the same plane and I would need to apply for a visa if I was staying for more than 10 days. Anyway, I went up to the Thai Embassy to get a visa for three months and flew out early October. My job there was as an Illustrator for their Sunday School material. Each morning I would have Thai lessons to enable me to communicate a little bit. It's a very difficult language as you can have the same word but a different meaning if you don't use the right tone and there are five different ones! There are diphthongs, and about 44 consonants to think about. People say English is difficult to learn but I don't know, I think Thai is very difficult.

In October, it's the rainy season in Thailand. It pours down heavily with rain and there is thunder and lightning too but the rain will fall for a short while and then stop. It's fascinating to see how the Thai's cope with this type of weather really. Motorbikes (that would often carry a whole family) would stop, pull over to one side, maybe stay under a tree or bridge for shelter and wait for the downpour to stop and off they all go again, and the heat (which I thought was very humid, but not English humid) would dry people off very quickly.

Eunice took me to lots of different places, Bangkok, a Thai cultural show, where we had a ride on an elephant (these are very sacred creatures to the Thai's), we visited people who lived in houses built on stilts because of the water around them, we went to the boat market, we took an overnight train to Chiang Mai, North Thailand, which I loved and we stayed at a Christian Guest House there. The city seemed to come to life at night, with a street market which was so lit up I forgot it was dark. It was very exciting and new! The Thai people like to treat you like a VIP, they are very good hosts. The whole visit was very educational and it was great to see where Eunice lived and worked. You would think that she was a Thai yourself because she is so fluent in Thai.

About a year later, Tim and I went to see my Mum and Dad and Tim asked them if he could marry me. To my shock they weren't keen. He was a teacher, we had been going out for years, he was a Christian, read his bible loads and even preached – what was wrong? I concluded they just didn't like him. They said to wait and apparently Mum said she didn't think he loved me enough. I was lost for words, very upset and angry.

So, Tim and I eloped and got married in Gretna Green, November 1991. And because we had just got everything together and 'ran off' we didn't exactly have anywhere to live. We stayed in Scotland for a week and eventually returned to his home town of Croydon. For 30 days we lived in the car. MacDonalds was our 'dining room/lounge', the library our 'reading room' and our bathroom was the 20p cubicles that you could find on the corner of some streets in Croydon. It was an art to 'wash' yourself – teeth and everything – before the timer ended and the door released. We later settled for a while and lived with his mother, Audrey.

Before Emma was born, I was cycling from Croydon to London Bridge to save money (it was over £100 a month for a train ticket). But I had a miscarriage, probably from the cycling because it was 14 miles there and 14 back so that's a lot for me. It was clearly too much for me so I went back to the buses and trains especially when I was carrying Emma.

Emma was born in Croydon, March 1994 and Alex was born in Bristol, July 1997. Emma and Alex were my two little miracles in my life - two shiny stars!

By November 1998, Emma was four and Alex was nearly one and a half but my marriage to Tim had sadly broken down. I stayed with Ruth and Ann for a bit who were a tremendous help during this heart-breaking time.

I went to stay with Chris (Curtis) who was now married to Helen, and had some time out with them. We had several chats which was good as Chris knew Tim from University (14 years earlier) and we had kept in touch over the years. Chris and Helen were very kind and gave me time and listened well and gently gave suggestions. Both Chris and Helen talked to both of us to try and help. They are a lovely couple and really give out to others a lot. (Chris is now the Chief Executive of Youthscape in Luton).

I had borrowed some money from a friend to buy a car, which was my life-line. My sister, Eunice, was home in England on furlough and I was living with her in Bristol - she suggested that if I had any problems with my car, I should take it to Martyn Clamp whom she trusted and always took her car to him when she was home in England. This I duly noted down especially as I was driving backwards and forwards from Bristol to Chippenham for work, Monday to Friday.

I had a temping post in Chippenham, in charge of the Purchase Ledger Department. But I was feeling so low, unwell with no appetite and losing loads of weight, it was just dropping off me. My concentration became poor and it was hard just to fill out forms and keep up with the work load in the office. I resigned from work and interestingly the company employed two people to do the same job that I was doing. I always said it was too much for one person.

I began to file for a divorce. I just wanted to be free of Tim but because I was the bread-winner and Tim was a house husband I had left the children with him. (I had begged him to get a proper job for several years but he never did). So, I asked the solicitor how to get my children back because it was so painful, not having them. Every time I thought about them it was like being run over by a bus. She said to continue regular access with Em and Alex and I could deal with the divorce first and then go to court for the children. But a bit later the solicitor suggested that both Tim and I went to Mediation and to take all the advice they offered.

All the legality of the divorce, finances and keeping good access to Em and Alex was becoming too much. I felt tormented that I had left Emma and Alex with their dad I should have taken them with me, they should be with their Mum. Tim didn't always make contact easy. It was a journey into a dark, frightening tunnel as this was new ground that I had never trodden on before. I was so grateful for my sisters,

Ruth, Eunice, and Ann who were very supportive. They all understood why I wanted to leave and tried all they could to help.

15 Something's Wrong

I had had several sessions of Christian Counselling which was, emotionally, hard going as you had to go through past hurts I had long since hidden but were relative to my now? There was a lot of digging deep, asking for forgiveness and praying as well as forgiving myself. I was so grateful for the time given to me by two ladies at my sister's church. It was almost like picturing my heart as a garden and the weeds had accumulated so much that it was quite stuffy, smelly and ugly in there. The effect of healing was amazing and a great load was shifted off my shoulders, which made my 'garden' clear of so many weeds. Everything was cut back, clear and fresh ready to start again. For so many years I worried about what people thought of me. That was a huge problem for me but now it's all gone! I was still searching for a way forward though. I thought 'Ok, so I have messed up. I can't see God wanting to use me now, not in this predicament, even if I've done an abundance of weeding in my garden! I was still damaged goods; but just remember:

Noah was a drunk
Abraham was too old
Isaac was a daydreamer
Jacob was a liar
Leah was ugly
Joseph was abused
Moses had a stutter
Gideon was weak
Samson had long hair and was a womaniser
Rahab was a prostitute
Jeremiah and Timothy were too young
David had an affair and was a murderer
Elijah was suicidal
Isaiah preached naked
Jonah ran from God
Naomi was a widow

Job went bankrupt

Peter denied Christ
The disciples fell asleep while praying
Martha worried about everything
The Samaritan woman was divorced, more than once
Zacchaeus was too small
Paul was too religious
Timothy had an ulcer
And Lazarus was dead!
(This is from a leaflet that sits on our fridge)

One day, I could see that several drivers behind me were flashing their headlights at me and motioned that one of my brake lights weren't working. I had already had it changed. I got back home and Eunice said I should take the car back to Martyn as there might be a loose connection or something. He was living at a different address but I did have his telephone number still from a previous car problem.

The next day, I took my car to him. He was very kind and we chatted while he fitted a new bulb. We had a lot in common and we were in similar situations. I was tired and needed to lean on something. The first thing I saw was his, very used, old looking car trolley jack. But it was black with grease on the handle bars and he said in a perturbed way "don't lean on the jack!" He was concerned I would get grease on my clothes not just my hands.

Thursday 3rd December 1998

I got back to Whitchurch and Martyn rang the landline and Eunice said "I think you've made a new friend there." We planned to meet at MacDonalds in Brislington the next evening. It was the 3rd December 1998. We didn't stay at MacDonalds but went to the Globe at Newton St Lowe, just outside Bath. We had a drink and chatted over where we grew up, people we knew and what we had been through. He then looked up and said "would you like to come and see the Christmas lights in Bath with me?" I replied "yes please!"

The streets were practically empty, the Christmas lights were pretty and gave me a sense of nostalgia. Having been brought up in Bath I had fond memories of Sue and I doing our Christmas Shopping when we were young and through to our teenage years. The air was chilly, not frosty or drizzly just a cold December evening. I asked Martyn what kept him going through his troubles and his reply was simply "God, my faith". This was the first time I really listened to someone talking about their own faith.

Martyn and I continued to keep in contact but we were a bit off and then on again as we were both in a place of hurting and it seemed too soon to get involved with each other.

Even though I had resigned from my position in Chippenham my health seemed to be getting worse. I had several bouts of flu or tonsilitis and a cough that lingered for weeks on end. With no appetite I felt tired, weak and weary. I missed talking to Martyn it was like we were holding hands to try and get through the dark tunnel.

There were many times when I felt like just giving up. Maybe, I was an awful sinner and this was my punishment? Where or when was all this going to stop, I kept asking God. I need help and I need it now Lord! If you can't answer me Lord, where can I get some help?

One day I was feeling so unwell with flu symptoms, Eunice was at work and I plodded around the house, passing the time away until she came home and I had some company. She had her graduation from Trinity College, Bristol the next day which she had invited me to, with Dad and a couple of other close friends. But during the night I felt worse than ever. The pains in my arms and legs were so bad I could hardly move. I wanted to get up and take some paracetamols but I really couldn't cope with the pain and felt tied to the bed. This was weird but I felt that I really needed to do something. The only thing I had next to me was my mobile and without too much trouble I dialed the home telephone number. It rang and rang and Eunice finally got up to answer it but just before she could pick up the handset I hung up. I then called out Eunice but she didn't hear me as she had gone in to the toilet. I waited until she came out and quickly shouted "Eun! Eun!" She popped her head around the door – great hair Eun! - and I looked at her and said that I felt really ill and didn't think I would make it to her service tomorrow and that I desperately needed some painkillers. She took my temperature. "Oh, my goodness!" she said "it's 104°F!". This was a bit unexpected and staggering! I didn't even feel hot. We weren't sure why it was so high – maybe it was just the flu - but she gave me some paracetamols and said that hopefully by drinking lots and taking the tablets this would bring my temperature down. I was still unwell in the morning so Eunice made some alternative arrangements as I couldn't go with her. Eun, very kindly, brought me a tray with a selection of drinks to get through while she was out. But I slept *all* the time she was out – I was so out of it, but it did me the world of good even though Eun was a bit cross that I hadn't drunk anything. Whatever it was, it came and went. During the next couple of days, the pains in my arms and legs subsided but I didn't have much of an appetite, it was just best to try and eat when I fancied something rather than nothing.

Martyn and I went to see one of his sisters and her husband, Hilary and Graham Steer. They clearly loved Martyn and only wanted the best for him. He has three sisters but Hilary was the only one who lived in Bristol. Both Hilary and Graham were good listeners, very kind, considerate, gentle and supportive. It was very clear that they both spent a lot of time in prayer and their love just overflowed for people.

Wednesday 27th January 1999

Martyn and I decided to part company and met for the last time to say 'good bye' and wish each other the best. It was hard but we knew it wasn't good timing. I was so upset but it was for the best. I would continue to try and get well again and concentrate on my children. Later that night I crawled into bed with Emma on one side and Alex the other. I cried quietly. I love these two children of mine; they are such a treasure. As I laid there, I thought I don't have any more strength left for the roller-coaster of life at the moment and prayed "Lord, do I need to be seriously ill to have some time out or something?" I hadn't been an active Christian for a while now and I knew I needed to get back on track because I couldn't live without Him. The counselling made me realise this. Life had become too difficult. But it was hard getting back on the right path; it was as if 'someone' didn't want me to make that move. Praying a quick prayer like that was rather bold of me I thought. I fell asleep thinking I need time; I just needed a break from everything.

WEEK ONE

Thursday 28th January 1999

In the morning, 28th January 1999, I woke with a thumping headache. It was a struggle to dress the children but Emma was a little more independent than Alex, as he was only 18 months old. I managed to get them some breakfast, but I needed help from Eunice as I just didn't feel well at all. I took some paracetamol but it wasn't moving the pain. Eun was upstairs trying to get ready for work (she had an office job at the OMF office while on furlough). I picked Alex up out of his high-chair and then .... there it was .... AHHHhhhhhhh! Pain in the neck now. I'm sure I've cricked my neck, I thought, and I could hardly bend down to Alex, who had filled his nappy, and I could hardly stand up straight. I called out to Eunice but she couldn't hear me. She was in a hurry and asking for her help would probably make her late. There was a door at the bottom of the stairs and it had a latch. I couldn't reach it. That's odd, I thought, I haven't had a problem reaching it before. I tried again. Nope, neither arm would lift up high enough. I then put my left hand under my right elbow to push it up just high enough to loosen the latch.

"Eun!!!!!" I cried.

"What is it now?" She replied, obviously flustered and I didn't blame her for that. I said "I'm sorry but I need help. I think I have cricked my neck." She came down not very happy with me. She said "well, take some paracetamol or something." I replied, exhaustedly, "I have, for a headache, but it's not working. But I can't lift Alex up and I think he needs his nappy changed" Ohhhhhh......I felt such a burden to Eunice but I needed her help and I wasn't making any of this up, my arms started to tingle with pins and needles. But thankfully Eunice began to realise that I wasn't well and came to the rescue!!

I may have interrupted Eunice's morning timetable but she came up trumps, she changed Alex, even though he objected a lot, and she got Em and Alex both into her car and I bundled in the back with them. I was whimpering, the pain was getting worse, it was awful and I couldn't have Alex sit on my lap or have Emma cuddle me. Both children couldn't understand why Mummy was upset and they couldn't comfort me by sitting on my lap or cuddling me. My breathing was affected now. I could only take short breaths because my whole rib cage hurt so much. Eunice became concerned that I had pins and needles in my hands and suggested dropping Emma off to school first. We could then drop Alex back to his dad's and then Eun would drop me off at the doctors, which was only a couple of minutes away. Good plan Eun! Emma was a little late but the teacher didn't bat an eyelid because she could see I was struggling. She told me to go home and rest. Tim took one look at me and said "what the heck is wrong with you?". I just replied that I didn't feel well and was going to the doctors. I was now happy that both Emma and Alex were in good hands.

Eunice dropped me off and as I didn't want to be an inconvenience to her any more that day, I said I would walk round to my friend, Ann Bristow, and see if I could stay there until she finished work at OMF. If Ann wasn't there, I would have to get a bus back home to Whitchurch.

I sat in the doctor's waiting room. They had only just opened the doors and I didn't have an appointment so the receptionist said I could wait until the doctor had a free 10 mins. I sat and whimpered – I have never been in so much pain and discomfort, not even in labour. The receptionist was kind and brought me a cup of water and said that she was sure a doctor would be free soon. I could hardly lift the cup up to my lips and I was a bit embarrassed about that so left it on the table. After what seemed an eternity but was only a few minutes the doctor called me in. He decided that I had trapped a nerve and gave me a prescription to get some painkillers and anti- inflammatory tablets. I accepted what he said and thought that he knew best. I walked across the road to the Chemist, got my tablets and slowly walked to Ann's (B).

It was a painful walk and a slow one. I thought that I was never going to get to Ann's house and I kept praying "please Lord, let Ann be there." Over and over again I said the same prayer. If Ann wasn't there, I didn't know what I would do.

Finally, Ann's (B) house arrived! I was about to knock and Ann opened the door and said "Oh, hello! I'm just about to go out shopping." I desperately asked if I could stay at her house while she was out as I didn't feel well. I was really, relieved when she said yes. Before she left, she asked if I needed anything and I asked for water for the tablets, which I took readily but with tremulous hands and I asked if I could use her phone to ring Eunice at work to let her know what the doctor said. All agreed and sorted and off Ann went as I sat and dozed. I was so very tired. I then thought I had better ring Eun to tell her that the doctor said it was just a trapped nerve.

16 Accident and Emergency WEEK ONE

Thursday 28th January 1999

'Ok, so I have Eunice's telephone number here so I'll go to the kitchen and use the phone' I said to myself. I stood up and stepped forward a little and to my horror what happened next was disturbing. My legs just gave way – almost in slow motion, they melted beneath me and I ended up on the floor on my knees. I was between the arm of Ann's (B) sofa and the arm of the arm-chair. 'What's happening?!' I asked myself, slightly panicking. 'It's just a trapped nerve the doctor said. So, at some point it will un-trap itself and I'll be ok'. I'll just put my elbows on the arms to lift myself up. Nothing happened except my elbows gave way and I was slipping to the floor. 'What sort of trapped nerve is this?' I began to ask. I still could feel my feet and pushed myself with my heels towards the middle of the lounge so that Ann wouldn't step on me when she came in the door. I wriggled and wriggled until I was in a safer position. But now I was stuck. I stared at the ceiling and the adrenaline rushed in – whatever this is, I *will* overcome it. It won't last, don't get in a flap, it's a trapped nerve. This is what kept going round in my head. I'll trust what the doctor said because they do know what they are talking about, so I don't need to make a fuss, just go with it for now.

I woke up cold and I was still on the floor but I was probably only asleep for 5 mins. I was getting extreme pain in the shoulder blades and the top of my neck and I only wished I could grab a cushion to soften the surface I was lying on. I could still wriggle but by now I couldn't feel, well, most of my body! I realised that I still had my jacket on and maybe that was causing the discomfort. With a great deal of determination, I wriggled the jacket off, I don't know how I did it but I did and nudged it many times to become like some type of cushion. I have no idea how that was possible looking back now.

All I had to do was wait for the tablets to work and Ann(B) to come back from shopping. Why wasn't she back? Was she buying everything in ASDA? For two and a half hours I waited and drifted in and out of sleep or a doze now and then and at last the front door key turned!! Was I pleased to see Ann (B)! She looked at me weirdly and chuckled "what are doing on the floor Chris?" The only reply I could give was "I can't get up". She told me to hold on while she got her shopping bags in and put away the frozen groceries quickly.

Ann came over to me and asked what had happened. And I explained how I had tried to get to the phone to ring Eunice but my legs gave way. She said "this doesn't sound like a trapped nerve; I'll try and get you back on the sofa". Ann grabbed under the arms and tried to pull me up but I was a dead weight and even at six and a half stone it was hard for Ann to get me back up to sitting on the sofa. I then felt sick and woozy and found it difficult to sit up straight. We chatted about what the doctor said and because I have good faith in the doctors, I trusted what he said but Ann was doubtful. Ann (B) laid me down and I just flumped there on her sofa totally helpless. By now I could only move my head and everything else felt numb and my back was very painful. I couldn't understand that if you were numb how you can still feel so much pain!? Ann rang Eunice to say that I couldn't feel anything now and Eunice said that she would call in on her way home not realising how bad I was.

At about 2.50pm Ann had to pick her children up from school. Ann said she wouldn't be long and thankfully she wasn't. I was still in pain and a lot of discomfort and it was then I was wondering and asking myself that maybe, this isn't a trapped nerve after all and why hadn't the tablets worked at all. This was now 6 hours from this morning's cricked neck moment. 4 o'clock and Ann rang Eunice again to say that she had better come now. Eun left work and got to Ann's by 5 o'clock. By this time Ann (B) was on the phone to the doctors who said to call an ambulance straight away. The ambulance arrived with flashing blue lights. The paramedics were careful to pick me up and take me into the ambulance where they took a while to sort me out and strap me in well before 'hitting the road'. Once I was 'packed' up we left Ann's house and we got to Bristol A&E by around 6pm. Eunice met me there.

It seemed a very long wait and because they thought I had done something to my back I was strapped to those awful orange blocks and unable to move them. I was in such pain. I was grateful for Eunice being there for the moral support and she tried to move the sticky tight tape that held me firmly to the blocks but she was worried she would do more harm and it was so taut she could barely move them anyway.

At long last I was sent for an X-ray but they said nothing was wrong. So, they took the blocks away much to my relief. They kept asking me what I thought was wrong with me and I kept replying that I thought it was a trapped nerve. They also asked if I was stressed but the only answer I could give to that question was "well, I am divorcing my husband at the moment" but other than that not much else. They lifted my arms up and then let go of them and, of course, they immediately plummeted to the trolley that I was lying on. They asked how my arms felt. They had stopped being tingly and after so many hours after my initial collapse my whole body felt heavy and numb. We waited until 10.30pm when the doctor said we could go home now. What!?!!?! That's ridiculous! I insisted that I couldn't move – did they not believe me?! Basically, no, I don't think he did! The doctor came and swung my legs around and then pulled me into a sitting position. This was so painful, I cried out and just crumbled as a nurse and Eunice tried to make me stand. Someone! Please believe me!

Eunice and I had moments where there were just the two of us, and we were wondering what was going on and why all the waiting. The wait seemed forever. We chatted about this and that. I confessed to my 'silly' prayer asking God if I needed to be seriously ill to have some time out. We decided you had to be careful what you pray for. I can't believe why I chose those particular words either. Couldn't I have asked God to just have time out? Why did I add 'seriously ill'? The words, kind of, fell out of my thinking but what a stupid thing to think. I felt awful and quite an idiot *and* embarrassed for praying such a prayer.

Friday 29th January 1999

There was a changeover of staff and thankfully at 1am, 29th January 1999, the doctors began to take me seriously. The doctor who took me seriously, we'll call him Dr Tim, and I am thankful for him coming on duty just at the right time and the right place. It was helpful that Eunice said she knew who he was, not sure how – church, maybe? Apparently, the doctors had a bet with Dr Tim because they didn't think anything was wrong with me but he was sure there was something serious going on. They put me on a drip, took blood and put a catheter in – I felt VERY relieved!

The doctor came with a little yellow clip-thing and said that one end had a pin and the other didn't. He wanted me to say when I could feel a sharp pin prick or the blunt bit. Eunice said I got most of it wrong. He tested my reflexes and muscle function; I flunked all the tests though. They asked what I was doing when this happened, was I stressed and had I been ill recently – questions, questions and no answers as to what might be wrong. The next test or exam was humiliating and I felt I really *lost* all dignity. They laid me on my side and pulled my knees up as far as they would go up towards my chin. The doctor said he was sorry that he would have to do this test but it was *really* important. He had his rubber gloves on and gently put his finger up my backside! Whatever is this for? I screamed inside my head. He kept asking me "squeeze my finger" and I kept saying "I am, I am!" He insisted more and said "Chris, this is *very* important, you must try harder" and I replied "but I thought I was!". I think by this time, I and the doctors realised that I was numb and nothing was working from my neck down. I felt demoralised and embarrassed after that episode.

I know that when you have children all your dignity goes out the window then but this was more intrusive and it was over that certain line of privacy. But they wouldn't have done it unless they really had to, to help them in their diagnosis.

There was more waiting, but a different sense of waiting because it was now clear that something was seriously wrong. Eventually, in the early hours of the morning the doctor booked me in for a CT scan and then around 3.30 a.m. did a lumbar puncture. I have heard of these but never knew anyone who had had one and certainly I had never had an LP myself. Eun, said, "Oh, Chris, it's a big needle! It will probably hurt". But I didn't feel a thing – not a sausage! Dr Tim told Eun that I would probably get a thumping headache after it and told Eunice that she should go home and try and get some sleep. He then said that they would send me to have an MRI scan in the morning. I think she was quite emotionally exhausted, washed out and totally tired.

By now, I was still lying on a trolley in A&E. There was a shortage of beds so they wheeled me right to the back of A&E where it was quiet. I wasn't the only person there so I wasn't alone. They dimmed the lights and all was quiet. I was worried that the nurses would forget that anyone was in this back area.

I looked around and stared at the ceiling, the curtains, the walls because there wasn't much else to do. Here I was, my whole body was under attack. I wanted and needed to survive whatever this torturous disease was that had taken over me.

When you get grit in your eye you want it out, "Get out! Get out!" is all I wanted to say to this 'grit' in my body. I finally fell asleep only to wake up to find that I still couldn't move. I was so upset but I tried to stop myself from crying because I knew I couldn't wipe my nose or tears. It was a horrible feeling. An awful claustrophobic feeling came over me because I had sunk down deep into the pillows and I couldn't move or get myself out. The reality of not being mobile hit me and I just couldn't believe what was happening. I felt vulnerable and so unprotected for what was ahead of me. The only protection I had right now were the 'cot rails' on each side of the bed to stop me rolling out. But I couldn't even roll if I wanted to!

A lady came up to me, I can't remember if she was a nurse or an admin person, but she said that she understood that I wasn't well but the BBC, Points West, would like to speak to patients stuck in A&E waiting for a bed and she asked if I was up for it. I said yes, thinking that if Martyn saw the news he would know where I was. Matthew Hill, who was the Health Correspondent for the BBC in the South West, and a camera man came up to my bedside. He was well mannered and simply asked my name, where I had come from, what had happened to me and how long had I been in A&E. I explained that I couldn't move after 6 hours of picking up my son because of what I thought was a crick in the neck. I told him that the nurses were very kind and had looked after me well. I was breathless when I spoke but I gave the facts that they wanted. The nurse beside my bed then told them that I had actually been in A&E for 16 hours!

8.30am came and I was taken down for an MRI scan. As they wheeled me back Eunice, Ruth and Will (Ruth's husband) were waiting for me. Ruth wondered what on earth had happened and helped me drink some water, but I could not swallow properly and choked on the water. So now, I couldn't roll over, couldn't wipe my nose, couldn't go to the loo and couldn't even sip water properly. This was scary!

There were several doctors around me now and one man, who didn't seem to be a doctor at all – he was a consultant, Dr Campbell – said that the MRI scan showed up an inflammation in the spinal cord in C1 &C2 (the first two vertebrae of the cervical spine) which controls temperature and movement, etc. The doctor said it was very rare and they were unsure of the prognosis but were hoping for a complete recovery. I think they were being positive but there was a dash of reality chucked in with their comments because I could be in the group that doesn't walk again and lives in a wheelchair. It would be a matter of time before they were clearer on my future prospects. The best place for them to move me to was Frenchay, North East of Bristol, because they were specialists in spine injuries and neurological disorders. They were a bit concerned about my breathing though as they got me to blow into the measuring tube and it only read 1. It should have read 7. So, they made sure the right people were in the ambulance to take care of me on the way to Frenchay. Ruth, Will and Eunice went on to Frenchay and met me at Ward 2.

We later learnt that Dr Tim won 7 pints! I was pleased for him because he took me seriously but I hope that drinking so much didn't make him drunk.

17 Frenchay Hospital

Friday 29th January 1999

The journey by ambulance wasn't an easy ride. It was very bumpy and noisy with equipment rattling around. I felt faint and the pain in my back seemed worse than ever but the ambulance people kept a good eye on me.

We arrived at Frenchay and I was unloaded. At last, I briefly felt some fresh air on my face and saw some blue sky, be it very short-lived but it was a wonderful feeling of normality outside this nightmare. I hadn't ever imagined that I could appreciate fresh air that much! I was pushed along this everlasting corridor with strip-lights on the ceiling whooshing past above my bed on wheels. I felt I was on an upside-down airport runway. Again, I was beginning to feel light-headed and as they parked me up in the space allocated for my trolley a nurse came over and said "Can I have some help here!" I'm not sure but I may have fainted or passed out, probably with sheer exhaustion at this point. I began to dream and was enjoying some peace when I was aware of a 'being' or a presence looking over me.

I opened my eyes and with a little fright realised that an actual person was looking over me. He had a kind face, young with round glasses and fair hair. I suddenly remembered that I was naked under this gown and didn't feel very presentable at all for any consultation. This kind face spoke! He said, "Hello, I'm Chris Halfpenny, you can call me Chris if you like." He was a Registrar Consultant and his boss, Dr Campbell, was a Neurologist Consultant. Chris proceeded to do all the tests that they had done on me in A&E: the pin- pricking, testing my reflexes and muscle strength. Again, I failed the assessment. He said "Please try and not fall asleep Chris, I need you to be awake for this." But by now, all I wanted to do was rest and have a really good, long sleep! The most embarrassing thing about all this was that I didn't have any control over my bowels and it got quite windy at times, I was very humiliated, but there was nothing I could do about it, so I just apologised. But Chris said it was fine and not a problem. Maybe, he didn't have a sense of smell?!

Ruth, Will and Eunice appeared. I had to keep the oxygen mask on as the nurse said I needed it. Will stayed with me while Ruth and Eunice went off to speak to the doctor. I was very confused. At A&E they had told me something about a rare disease but I couldn't retain the information so I wasn't sure what was wrong and if there was a name to this illness or trapped nerve. Will asked if he could do anything for me. Because I felt lifeless, I asked him to rub my fingers so that I could try and at least feel something or that he could stimulate some movement in my muscles.

When my sisters came back, I asked what did the doctor say. They said that I had a rare disease called Transverse Myelitis and was paralysed from my neck down. At the time only 1 in 4 million people got this awful disease. I had a 33% chance of recovery. Which meant that a third of people who get T.M. recover fully, another third only half recover and the remaining third don't recover at all. The treatment for this disease was to put me on a high dosage of steroid in a syringe that would "drip-feed" into my veins. They did warn me that if I didn't move anything within the next two weeks then that could be a sign that I wouldn't move at all. They estimated that this would be my home for about six months. If I couldn't move in six months, how was that going to work out? Especially as Eunice and I were house-sitting on a short term basis. With all this new information I still had a problem processing details; I had to ask my sisters to repeat things a couple of times so that I could understand what I was up against. I did realise, of course, that this was going to be a dramatic change to my life, it was a shock and devastating to say the least. It was too much to take in so, for now, I decided to just accept that I would be in hospital for a while, rest a while and everything would be ok. My brain said it would try and work this out later. I would sleep in the hope that with each resting moment some healing would be going on inside me and that it was just a matter of time before I turned the corner towards some improvement.

Eunice told me that after she had left me several hours earlier, she couldn't sleep knowing that her sister was in hospital paralysed. She wanted to speak to someone but at 4am no-one was going to be awake. Eunice waited until a reasonable time, about 8 am I think, and rang Ruth and just burst into tears spurting out and trying to speak out the words that Chris is in hospital paralysed. Eventually, Ruth got out of Eunice exactly what she was trying to communicate and a wave of shock eventually went around the family. I didn't mean for Eunice or Ruth to have this worry but we are a very supportive, loving and caring family. We would do anything for each other.

I was tired, as well as Eunice, and it was decided to leave me in peace to catch up on some sleep and to let Eunice do the same.

There I was, a bump on a log in the H.D.U. (High Dependency Unit). I couldn't even scratch my nose! My mind travelled and buzzed with how all this was going to work out. My biggest relief was that the children were safe with Tim and I knew they were being cared for and their daily routines could continue.

I shouldn't have prayed that prayer "Lord, do I need to be seriously ill to have some time out or something?" What a stupid prayer! What was I thinking? Well, I wasn't thinking properly at all. No-one wants to be seriously ill. I was cross with myself but didn't have a great deal of energy to be really, angry with myself. I had to sleep, I told myself, and then all will be well. Yeah, like that's going to happen! But then I thought, I'm not leaning on that Jack in the garage now – who do I lean on for this kind of crisis? In this situation, most people would ask God why? Why me? But I wanted to ask God a different question. What am I going to do now Lord? Why has this been allowed? Then I realised that my 'garden' had been neglected and the weeds had grown back and I shouldn't have prayed that prayer! And someone did say to me that this was from the devil. Maybe, I had given him permission for this to happen. I don't know! Too many questions and no-one to answer them for me. But in all honesty, this time out was good in a strange way, not the suffering but the realisation that my 'garden' was in a mess and I hadn't been including Jesus in my life for some time now. I really was paralysed without Jesus.

Later that evening a nurse came up to me and said, "I have a telephone call for you – a Martyn Clamp. Would you be ok if he came to see you?" I said "Yes, that's fine" but I had broken up with him the day before and was no good for anyone right then. A bump on a log. He took about five minutes to arrive, so I am guessing he found out where I was and was already on the hospital premises. He came up to the side of my bed and said "What's all this about?" I didn't know what it was about but I did know that I was a heavy lump not going anywhere fast. He said he had been thinking and had walked miles and miles to find me and he wanted me to wait for him, he wanted to be with me! This was so sweet of him, but now that I was unable to move, I think he had better have a serious think about what he really wanted. He stayed a while as we chatted and caught up with what had been happening the last couple of days and then he kissed me on my forehead and left.

18 My New Home

Saturday, 30th January 1999.

Eunice had started a diary that was kept on my bed-side table which was helpful when you wanted to know who had been in to visit and was there space for others to come and stop by as the number of people around your bed was limited. The first visitors today were Eunice, Dad, Mum, Steve, Andy, Sue and Ruth.

As I was the 'newbie,' my bed was placed near the nurses' station. When the next new house mate arrives then I would be moved down. So, the ward had its own line-up and care system. Because I couldn't move at all I was put on a Ripple Bed. It really did ripple, up and then down the bed. It's not a water bed but at times it felt like one, no, it's basically an air bed which is connected to a small motor/pump contraption pushing a cloud of air within the rubber bed casing. It constantly hums but totally out of tune!

Unfortunately, with each ripple it set me off with 'breaking wind' and I had to learn to cope with the embarrassing body odor from my bowels and so did my visitors. Everyone seemed to cope quietly and admirably; all the while I was desperately hoping all my guests didn't have a sense of smell.

It had been several days since I had opened my bowels and I was panicking as to when and how it was going to happen. It will end up being a thunder storm surely!? (underneath, I felt totally humiliated)

Then, of all the times, something began to happen – it was painful and distressing. It didn't register what was going on, the brain signals weren't working and got very confused. Mum, Dad and Steve were still around me and I said "Oh, no. Something is happening – I don't know what but it's really painful." Steve responded and called someone and the nurse ushered everyone out for a moment or two while she sorted me out. Sure, enough it happened and I was humiliated. How do other patients in the ward manage with this problem? But the nurse was so matter of fact she made me feel at ease, at least a bit, considering my unfortunate situation. I have said before that if you have had children your dignity has already gone out of window; this was just another line of business in the personal hygiene department, another level of losing your dignity.

Once I was cleaned up and the air-fresheners squirted, visiting time resumed – if anyone was up for it!?

Family left and meal times came and went, medication topped up and a routine began to form. I couldn't help with answering the telephone, I couldn't help with the dusting or cleaning floors and I couldn't get up and watch the television, wherever it was based. So really all I had were my thoughts. I waited and waited for the next excitement of the day and learnt it was better NOT to look at the clock.

I tried praying again, but was lost for words. "Lord, all I can do is wait to see what happens next". But my prayers seemed to be lost in thin air.

Sunday came and more visitors. Eunice, Sue and her husband Jem, their three young children – Stephen, Emma and Daniel, and also Ruth and then Martyn. It was kind of my family and friends to come and visit as Frenchay wasn't the nearest hospital for many.

I wanted to know what was going on in the outside world, like the weather! Which you could almost work out from what they were wearing, thick coats, hats and gloves. Any important news going on in the world? And were Emma and Alex, ok?

Monday 1st February 1999

"Uncle" Ian came on Monday and he brought in a potted plant – a purple, very cute violet. I was amazed how the word was getting around so quickly. Ann came in next and her comment she wrote in the diary was that the nurse inside her said "Can each visitor make sure she has a drink!" Quite often when the tea trolley came around, I was given a cup of coffee as requested and it was left on the table. But I had no ability to pick the cup to enjoy a hot drink nor was I able to drink water by myself. So, they were wasted because I had no assistance which would have been helpful. The 'helpers' were so busy I didn't always like to ask and be an inconvenience to anyone. But the nurses and doctors insisted that I should be drinking water for now anyway. The steroids made me so hungry and thirsty but the adverse effect of that was my tummy bloated out like a balloon.

After lunch-time, everyone settled down to an afternoon siesta. The lights went off and everyone went quiet and still. The nurses would come and puff the pillows up for me and I would lie there and close my eyes. I imagined I was next to a stream, warm sun shining on my face, sun beams drifting in the air, bees harmlessly buzzing around, green grass and pretty daisies swaying in the gentle breeze. I was soaking all this up on many afternoons, it was a good place to be, my happy place. All I wanted to do was rest and restore my soul in this peaceful place. Yes, restore was the word. That said it all. Psalm 23 came to mind every afternoon and it was soothing and gave me peace.

Psalm 23 (New International Version)

"The LORD is my shepherd, I lack nothing.

2 He makes me to lie down in green pastures, he leads me beside the still waters,

3 He refreshes my soul. He guides me along the right paths for his

name's sake
.[4] Even though I walk through the darkest valley, I will fear no evil, for you are with me; your rod and your staff, they comfort me
.[5] You prepare a table before me in the presence of my enemies. You anoint my head with oil; my cup overflows
.[6] Surely your goodness and love will follow me all the days of my life, and I will dwell in the house of the LORD forever."
(This is the reason for putting a picture of still waters on the front cover).

Chris Halfpenny, the Registrar Consultant came to visit to check on me. I said I was keeping positive but I had a few questions. He asked if it was anything he could answer. I took a pause and asked if he believed in Jesus and to my surprise he said yes! So, I asked him why do these things happen to people like me. He said he honestly didn't know the answer to that question. It was good to chat about Christian things with him. He went to church with his wife and children and yes, there are many things that happen in the world that we just don't know the answers to. Why *do* people get hurt or ill?

Chris had to get on. So, I had a little chat with God and said that if I didn't recover then He had to show me what I could do to make life live able and worthwhile from a wheelchair. People do find out what they are good at and that flair can grow and mature into something that gives them purpose. Joni Erickson is a very good example; Jennifer Rees Larcombe another, and many others.

So, after going round in circles trying to fix things myself but knowing that I couldn't, I eventually got to a point of accepting things and whispering "Whatever happens Lord, I'll go with it or rather go with you". I'll let go and let God. We are all unique and each day we have chances to grow as a person and to learn lessons through our struggles; we can then empathise with others who experience similar situations by understanding all the emotions that come in these circumstances and we can love them, befriend them and be compassionate.

Eunice came in the evening and later Martyn, who said "It was nice to help you with the drink but get your hair washed!". John and Penny from my last place of work in Chippenham, came in the evening and they were shocked, not only by my condition but also the new hair style – I think I needed a mirror or maybe it was better not to look. By 8.15pm Ruth and Will arrived and managed to arrange a telephone call to Tim and Emma. Oh, it was *so lovely* to hear Emma and she was so excited about doing P.E. tomorrow, bless her. She had little knowledge or no understanding of where I was or what was happening.

Tuesday, 2nd February 1999

In the morning the cleaners would arrive with their brooms, buckets and mops, sprays and cloths. I wanted them to feel appreciated and often would say "The floor looks lovely!" Some would chuckle and chat as they carried on their work and others would just smile and move on. Some of them became familiar faces and it was a great opportunity to ask what it was like outside. The current weather forecast was frosty. But I was very snug where I was and didn't have to experience that frost out there.

Ann (B), my friend (in whose house I collapsed) came to visit with her son, Connor (he was about the same age as Alex – 20 months +). Also, Sue and Ann arrived. But they were all in trouble for coming outside of visiting hours – ooops! But at least I had had my hair washed and was feeling very refreshed.

I had a moment with Jesus – I know He was watching over me and I had an overwhelming sense of peace and extra strength in coping with this disease. This real sensation seemed to come from nowhere, but it was an amazing sense of His realness. It was a sense of being carried. It didn't stop the pain or the fever. But then, all of a sudden, I could wiggle my left two fingers – the little finger and the next one to it (normally called the wedding ring finger). Wow, this could be the start of my recovery, I thought with excitement.

I also had a visit from my previous boss – also given the 'uncle' title. Uncle Charles. He was a very respected man. He had a good sense of humour and knowledge. He used to be in the army but I'm not sure what as, or rather I just can't remember. He wrote jokingly in the diary "Pull yourself together!" – that was Uncle Charles! Then Pam Richards came to visit me from Eunice's church and she said that it was terrible when you have to do something so drastic just to get a decent rest, not that you can call a hospital a restful place. And she told me to be nice to the nurses.

Pam came with Pearl Aitkien (OMF). She said they had got lost trying to find the ward and must have walked miles. She couldn't believe that I was enjoying hospital food but then compared with Eunice's cooking maybe it was good!

19 The Physio Squad

By now I was out of ICU and on a different ward. The Physiotherapists were on my case almost immediately. If I'd known what they were about I would have shouted "don't let them in!". Anyway, the first day the girls arrived in their uniform and started to try and move my arms and legs gently. This was to give my brain a nudge that this is what my limbs are supposed to do. A gentle reminder in a way. Each day they came to prompt those movements. It was so painful though, but I had to try. With each move I let out an "ow-ow-ow!" It had the same painful ordeal as if someone was bending your little finger backwards too much. The arms felt the same as well as the wrists and legs, everything. I had muscle wastage so my legs and arms were very thin. I just hoped that in their enthusiasm none of my bones would snap.

The physiotherapists began to threaten me with taking me to the gym but I felt so unwell, I really just wanted to be left alone and battle with the pain in my back and the sweats. And I so wanted a shower and to wash my hair, I was not interested in the gym!

Getting ready for a night's sleep was hard. Because by the end of the day the pain in my back was hard to cope with. Through the day I regularly asked the nurses to puff the pillows up because I just wanted something soft to lie on. I realised after a while that the pillows weren't the problem; it was just the pain in my back around the shoulder blades. There was no comforting that pain except for the stronger painkillers. Before the lights were turned out they would go around with the medicine trolley and they would ask me if I needed any painkillers. The answer was always YES PLEASE! Some patients and nurses called one of the drugs "jungle juice." I don't know if they meant Diazepam or what? If I said the pain was ten out of ten, they would give me something much stronger which would knock me out in minutes. It was so good to get some sleep. I am now sure that you've picked up that I was in a lot of pain and just in case you hadn't – did I mention about the pain? I'm not sure but a bed of nails may have helped and diverted the pain elsewhere? Of course, some days were better than others but the painful days were very exhausting and wearing and all I wanted to do was blank it out and sleep so that I wouldn't have to cope with the pain or try and manage it.

20 Life in the Fast Lane

Mark and Cathy came to visit from my previous job in Chippenham. They congratulated me on becoming a TV star and felt the need to come and meet me in person. I showed them the finger dance that I could do – it should be in the Olympics! But for now, it was just a good party trick.

Ruth and Will also came but while Mark and Cathy were by my bed-side they popped to the hospital restaurant for a drink. Ruth worked for BIME (Bath Institute of Medical Engineering but now it is called Designability) and they had a special project today to make a Flat Touch Switch which was connected to a Walkman so that I could turn it off and on with my elbow. What a BRILLIANT invention! Ruth left a message in the diary: "Loads of love, your Secretary Sister Ruth and Company Chairman Brother-in-law, Will XXXX".

Now I had a party trick that I could perform with my fingers, I felt very encouraged because the doctors did say that if I didn't move within the first two weeks then I would probably never move. I felt that I was on a spring board for getting better and maybe I will get a release date for good behaviour?

I had flowers and an amazing array of get-well cards. There were several strings above my bed to hang the cards on. I couldn't count them!

Eunice would pop in practically every day, which was exhausting for her, I'm sure. In my mind I was thinking she likes being needed but actually she had enough on her plate and probably didn't need to come in every day. I should have told her.

By now, I had more movement in my hands and feet. Although it all seemed very slow but very encouraging and invigorating.

WEEK TWO

Thursday 4th February 1999

The physiotherapists came in with a flat bed with several straps and, what looked like, a metal plate at the foot end. It was also characteristic of something out of a torture chamber! They slid me onto the flat bed and said that because I had been lying down for so long, they needed to start getting me used to being in the upward position again. Once they had strapped me in, they pressed the button on the control panel and the bed began to slowly tilt upwards and forwards. After just a couple of seconds I began to feel woozy so the girls suggested that they would go slower but they wanted to see if I could go further. A little more and a little more they pushed but I couldn't take it and said "I'm going to be sick – quick – bowl!" Not a good workout and I certainly didn't like the sensation it gave me. I never imagined that this could be a problem. It had only been about a week since my body had broken down but it was going to take a while to fix it back together. How long it takes just depends, it could be a quick recovery or much longer, according to how much time is needed for the body to heal itself and recover.

While I was in hospital, I had several UTI's (urinary tract infection), so this meant I had to have more fluids. Water is very boring and not that easy to swallow! When they came to empty my 'bag' the smell was a knock out! These infections were very common with a catheter.

Another visit from a friend from Chippenham. Brian wrote in the diary, "You'll do anything for a bit of attention! Whatever next?" He did say to take it easy though. Ann (B) came with her husband, Bart, and her three children, Shannon, Kerri and Connor. It was lovely to see them and on leaving she said "Hope you don't feel too tired after the tiresome trio!" Sometimes, when visitors came, I was often lost for words and it felt a bit overwhelming especially if I had had a demanding time in the gym trying out the latest gymnastic technics.

There were two ladies opposite me. One hardly spoke at all but the next one along was very pleasant, friendly and chatty. The chatty one, sorry but I have forgotten her name now, said she had been in for a while. I can't remember why she was in but she walked with sticks and did look very thin and pale. She said to me that when I was up for it, she would race me to the coffee shop downstairs. I said "You're on!".

The quiet patient had Multiple Sclerosis (M.S.). We'll call her Shirley. I felt sorry for her because she was very stiff, couldn't get out of bed and could hardly talk. She often struggled to call out "Nurse! Water!" and if no-one heard her, I would press my button for her because she couldn't even grab the switch/button. She had a brother who would visit once a week, on a Saturday, from Exeter. The other days she sat alone during visiting time – very sad to watch.

Friday 5th February 1999

Ann, my sister, kindly visited me again, and I told her I had been on the tilting bed as the physios wanted me to get used to being vertical. Ruth & Will also came in the afternoon at the same time as the physiotherapists and the Consultant, Chris Halfpenny. Jo, the Physiotherapist, was moving my arms and legs (ow-ow-ow!) and had elevated my feet onto a pillow. Ruth felt my feet and said they were cold. Chris told Ruth and Will that people DO make a full recovery from this condition. So, I thought of planning a football match. On this same day, Judith, one of the nurses, said I had received a letter. She had to open it for me – as with any other post – as my hands were unable to hold anything at this point. She said it was a letter from the BBC, who wanted to visit and do an interview. But I wasn't feeling well enough. So, she contacted them to say no.

Saturday 6th February 1999

Today, was a special day because Sue arrived at 3.30pm closely followed by Eunice, Emma and Alex. Alex was a bit overwhelmed to begin with and clung onto Eun; probably because he wasn't used to seeing me connected to tubes in a bed in a strange place. It was lovely to be re-united but strange that I couldn't cuddle them, I just couldn't lift my arms up to put around them. But it was very special to have them there with me.

Thankfully, I could move more and progress seemed to be coming along faster than I expected. My second eldest brother, Dave, came to visit me. He is a man of very few words, very kind and caring though. I explained the mysteries of the rippling bed and threatened a pillow fight next time he visited.

At 8.50pm news came through that my younger brother, Andy and his wife, Kate, had had a baby girl, born at 5pm today – Emily. Mum and daughter were doing well but no news of the dad!! I imagined Andy skipping down the corridors or cuddling his new baby.

I was cheerful and felt positive for a good recovery. 'I'm going to beat this' I would tell myself. I was now able to be propped up even if I still felt drunk and wobbly. This was going to be an adventure of a new, more appreciative life and my aim was to walk again however painful those work-outs became.

Monday 8th February 1999

Eunice, my P.A. came in this morning. She was taking care of all my paper work and had to be given Power of Attorney for me, which I was very grateful for, especially as my maximum ability to write was to form two lines to make a cross on paper and even gripping a pen was difficult.

People were kind and the visitors still kept coming. I know that for several family members it was easily, a 60-mile round trip. Even my eldest brother, Paul and his wife, Chris, came across from London to visit!

The tilting bed came again that day and we were not good friends and not really on talking terms. It doesn't talk, it isn't friendly or comfortable; it just made me feel faint and sick, no apologies for its behaviour, none whatsoever. The physiotherapists said that I should be patient and in time there will be a breakthrough. But I can't lie, there was a barrier between us and I couldn't see how it could be broken down. One of us would have to give in or we would have to go our separate ways. The other problem that day was a silly cold that was hanging around and spots on my forehead which the doctor thought might be chicken pox. Thankfully not, though, as the spots were only on my face and were probably a reaction to the steroids.

Martyn came to visit and I asked him if he could do me a really big favour. He graciously said "anything" before knowing what I was going to ask him. I said with a pent-up giggle "could you help me blow my nose please?" To my utter surprise his reply was "yes" but I had such a stuffy nose it got quite messy without going into too much detail. He then said, with a brave smile "Do I know you well enough to be doing this?". It was tricky but with mission accomplished I felt much more comfortable and I knew Martyn could probably do most awkward things – I always imagined he could because he's a mechanic!

Tuesday 9th February 1999

Ann, my sister, came in regularly which was gracious of her. She was so willing to help with my hygiene needs and would encourage me on my movement skills. Ann was helpful when I wanted my hair washed. She was able to find a bowl and a jug. I can't remember if she had help to move me but she needed my head off the end of the bed, at the head end of course so that she could pour the water over my head and the water would fall into the bowl. It was an amazing sensation – oh – I was so grateful! I can't really explain how therapeutic it was to feel that warm water on my head. It was such a treat. Ann said I didn't even have to pay on my way out!

One of the first things the physiotherapists gave me was a wooden, long, battered walking-stick. They placed it in front of me and I thought they were very silly to give me such equipment when I couldn't even stand. But that wasn't the purpose of this cane. I had to hold it and lift it above my head. Well, to begin with I couldn't even lift it. It may have been very light to them but it seemed to weigh a couple of tons to me!! But the more I had a go the more I could lift it and then a bit higher and higher still. So, my movements increased, mainly upper chest and arms. I could even hold a beaker of water and feed myself some ice-cream. I was also able to feed myself a chicken sandwich, a little chocolate mousse; and I even managed to hold my coffee drink! So, I must have been getting stronger!

At night-time, although, numb, I got a lot of cramp and had to get someone to straighten or rub my legs. It was an uncomfortable weird feeling. Because I couldn't move or turn over in bed, the nurses would come at regular intervals through the day and turn me over – flip me over from the left to right or right to left, using the bed sheet. One night, while flipping me over the sheet ripped and we couldn't stop laughing! They thought I must have gained a load of weight during the day – or was it actually a really old bed sheet?

The physios suggested to me that it was good to have a plan each week and a goal, so my aim before the end of the week was to sit in a wheelchair.

Wednesday, 10th February 1999

Wow - Eunice came with Emma!! What a lovely surprise!! I was just about to be wheeled down to x-ray, so Emma had a ride next to me on my bed. I cried with tears of joy just to see her and have her by my side. Thank you, Eun! Emma had done pictures for me – so sweet! We had a precious time together and it didn't matter whether her visits were short or long. Seeing her go was difficult. I knew she couldn't stay, that would be so impractical and definitely not allowed. I wasn't sure if Em felt the same or even if she understood yet what was happening to her Mum.

WEEK THREE

Friday, 12th February 1999

Today, the Physios were trying to get me to sit up on the edge of the bed, which was easier said than done. There was one on my right and the other on my left and they propped me up and then let go. Funnily enough, I couldn't hold myself and either swayed forward, backwards or to one side; so, it was a good thing that I had a person on each side. They were humorous girls/ladies which was good because it meant that I could laugh at myself and then have another go. At this point I felt as though I was still such a long way off from a complete recovery. I would get impatient and frustrated with myself – I want to get up and go and do!

Some nights, I just couldn't get comfortable and I hated being tilted onto my left side. One night the nurses 'flipped' me over but, unfortunately, about ten minutes later I said I wasn't comfortable and could I be moved again. There was a nurse with the main nurse, this time, who was training, and just before they moved me again, I said, "oh no, I have cramp in my left leg, please could someone rub it – do anything!" The, staff nurse (whoever she was), explained my condition to the other nurse while she rubbed my leg. I calmed down and they moved me onto my back and off they went again. I think, at this point, they thought they had seen the last of me for the rest of the night but then I pressed the help button again - I had to call them because my arm was wet with blood. In the excitement of the 'flipping' activities my arm cannular had accidentally been pulled out. It would have hurt normally, but I hadn't felt any pain at the time, just a wet feeling around my arm. The nurses on duty were not able to put it back in or put a new one in, they had to get someone qualified to insert a new one. It was in the middle of the night and I think they got an anesthetist to come and insert the cannular.

Messages, by e-mail or telephone, kept coming in and a constant supply of confectionary too. The cards kept coming in too which I really appreciated. To learn that so many people were thinking and praying for me was a great comfort, especially when I didn't feel up to praying myself. I felt as though other people's prayers were carrying me. What amazing friends and family I have who are giving so much support. There were *several* lines of strings above my bed now which held the lovely display of so many different, beautiful get-well cards. I had asked for a picture of me, Emma and Alex to be put up there in the middle of the cards. This was to remind me how I used to be, and hopefully it would urge me on and give me an aim each day towards getting back to being me.

At night time I would look up at the array of cards and there was a gap. Through this space shone the night light. Most of the ward lights were turned off but the middle one was left on during the night and I was just under it. The next day I asked for someone to move the cards along so that the light didn't shine in my face and keep me awake. But the shift didn't make any change to that beaming light it just didn't want to be shut out. So, I turned this into a positive. It reminded me that Jesus was shining His light on me and watching over me, even during the nights. I was also reminded that He really did love me and that He had paid a big price for me.

I had my arms put in Neoprene splints which gave me more support and the plasterers came in to see me – not to plaster the walls – but they made a cast of my right leg. When it had dried enough, they got a saw to cut the cast in half so that it could be put on and taken off – scary business – I was so nervous that the electric saw was going to cut my skin or worse still cut my whole leg off! This spare leg of mine had to be put on at night so that I wouldn't get a dropped ankle, but I didn't process this instruction very well or the importance of it; I couldn't reach anyway and the nurses would forget and so would I. It was more off than on.

For 45 minutes I managed to sit in a normal chair. After that length of time, I was in pain and very uncomfortable. My bony bottom was painful and sore; my back was tired and couldn't really hold myself up straight. BUT I did it, even if it was only 45 minutes – that was a milestone for me.

Every time the nurses or physios wanted to move me out of bed, they weren't allowed to lift me themselves. To move me they brought in a crane! I felt like a sack of potatoes being lifted up by that contraption, and the operation was hideously painful, especially for my back and neck. It was horrible. That crane was another piece of the hospital equipment that I wasn't friends with.

Several days later I was taken to the gym and this was planned to become a daily ritual, but not every day did I feel up to it. One day, I felt so terribly unwell I asked to be left in bed, my head was thumping like a bass drum.

But they didn't let me stay. They were bullies – but ones that only meant well; I think it was part of their job description.
Every manoeuvre was painful on this day. They would move

my legs and arms in the hope that my brain would remember those movements but I was a very reluctant team member that day.

Martyn visited me nearly every day and when he saw me sitting in the chair, he was amazed at the progress I was making. He brought in a specially wrapped up rose that day and took a photo of me sitting up and holding it.

The daily routine included the nurses checking all 'obs' (observations) and the phlebotomist visiting, who apparently was nick-named 'Dracula' (not nice!) to draw blood to be tested. My white blood cell count was up to 17, which they said was high and probably caused by the steroids. But I didn't really understand and I trusted them to get my bloods to the right number of counts.

Now that I could sit up for 45 minutes in a chair, the nurses decided it would be good if I had a shower because I could then sit on a seat in the wet-room and wash myself. I was actually scared of going to the bathroom because it was out of my new comfort zone but at the same time, I couldn't imagine anything better.

After a crane lifting session to sit me in a wheelchair, off we rolled to the wet-room. Once my clothes were discarded to one side and I was slid onto the shower chair the warm water began to rain on me. Wow! This was amazing. I would say 'lush'! I was able to have a go at washing myself which was a great leap forward. The nurse said that while I was safely sat there, she would pop out to see what was going on as someone seemed to be calling for help. So, there I was, sitting, waiting for a towel and clean clothes. I waited some more and some more. I had no idea what the time was or how long I had been there, but the nurse had clearly forgotten about me. Eventually, someone popped their head round and said "oh, sorry!" but I called out and said that I was waiting for the nurse to come back with some towels. She knew which nurse it was and said she would go and find her. At last, she came back with towel and clean clothes and apologised profusely because she really had forgotten me. But I was so relieved to see her it didn't matter anymore.

Saturday, 13th February 1999

It's been three weeks now and I have come a long way. Even though I am frustrated with myself, Eunice reminded me about:

Romans ch 5 v 3 & 4*:* (New International Version)
"3Not only so, but we also glory in our sufferings, because we know that suffering produces perseverance; 4 perseverance, character; and character, hope".

Today, not only did Paul and Chris come to visit again but also Sue my sister and her daughter Emma, Ruth plus Emma and Alex! Emma and Alex were happy teasing each other and at times Emma sat on my bed drawing on paper that Ruth had brought in. Sue drew round Alex's hand in my diary. It seemed a very noisy visiting session. But the gift of family is awesome.

That evening was quiet with no visitors – I had had them all earlier in the day. I needed to rest and I settled down to listen to the Corrs on a CD that Martyn had lent me. As I closed my eyes, I tried not to open them to see what the time was. Clock watching was a big mistake. I had to train myself not to look. The more I tried not to look the more I wanted to. This was hard work really – it was like being busy but not doing anything. That was it – I was busy just doing nothing, nothing at all! I think there's a song about that but the Corrs didn't have it on their CD.

Sunday, 14th February 1999

Not such a good morning. I did not feel well at all. Those sniffles were back, but apart from that I was moving more. Picking out tissues from the tissue box was good physio. It's a simple task but not when you're learning to co-ordinate your fingers and thumbs like a child.

The afternoon wasn't very peaceful. I had a new neighbour – we'll call her Denise. She moaned about everything and she argued loads with her visitors. Not good! I couldn't work out what was going on.

Thankfully, Ruth and Will appeared armed with jelly babies! Party time!! Unfortunately, they didn't help the coughing so Ruth got me some Tunes.

Monday, 15th February 1999.

They, whoever 'they' are, changed my ripple bed to a different one which was much better on the behind! I hadn't paid more for it or anything – maybe it was for good behaviour that they upgraded my bed.

That night was rough, I became distressed, uncomfortable and the coughing got worse. I was thinking that this was a nightmare on top of a nightmare. I was convinced that the end was near. It was a scary day because I really thought that I was going to die and with each coughing fit my mind was asking 'was this my last breath?'. In between the coughing fits my mind travelled fast wondering where would I really go if I did die. I am sure if you were in my position, you would probably be panicking unless, you were 100% of where you were going. But because I believe in Jesus I knew where I was going, I was sure of my destiny, just not sure if I was ready.

Tuesday, 16th February 1999.

Ann, my sister, arrived to help wash my hair which clearly wasn't going to happen that day. It was 10am and she found me propped up with an oxygen mask. They had put a nebuliser on me earlier but it just made me cough more. A nurse was pumping IV antibiotics into my right arm. It was a 'blip' a little 'set-back'. The doctor organised an x-ray which came to my bed – a very impressive mobile unit which I had never seen before. The cough was a chest infection. Instead of the physiotherapists taking me out on my gym date they came to me and tried rattling me! The idea was to shake my lungs, giving my chest some help to jiggle the phlegm up and out.

This chest infection was delaying my proper gym sessions and my movement improvements and I didn't want this. I wanted to get out! That's quite a mouthful if you say it out loud: "movement improvements".

Ann talked to the doctors, who were considering the possibility of moving me over to H.D.U. (High Dependency Unit). She hoped to talk to them later about their decision.

Later, Eunice came with Alex, and Ann went to check on what the doctors had decided. Alex was much more confident on this visit and wasn't so shy this time. They both stayed for about an hour, but because I felt so unwell – I was really worn out – Eun decided to take Alex back home.

Eunice came back later around 5.45pm and by then I was in great pain from a headache and neck ache. The doctors decided that I was ok enough not to be moved to H.D.U. and I was pleased at not being moved as the pain in my head and neck were the worst they had ever been. I was given a strong painkiller which made me doze on and off, but I needed moving a few times to try and get me comfortable.

At 7.20pm Ruth and Will arrived and joined Eunice at my bedside. The 'bed gang' tonight was good company and comforting to have by my side. Ruth had an e-mail from John, one of the managers from my job in Chippenham and Graham Vincent who I used to work with at Bath University. Ruth also gave me a cassette tape of the Corrs which Jonathan (Ruth and Will's son – my nephew) had got for me.

Apparently, it was quite cold outside but thankfully it was warm and cosy in the ward. By the time the 'bed gang' left I was feeling more comfortable.

Wednesday, 17th February 1999

Ann arrived and gave me a much-appreciated blanket bath. I was still unwell but continuing to improve with my oxygen level, and the antibiotics were beginning to work. The Physios came and battered me but it did help quite a bit. A simple shake can make such a huge difference. Ann said that I was looking pale but not as distressed as yesterday but my headache was still bad. I was given an injection and I'm guessing it was something to relieve the pain. I was 'nil by mouth' still and the doctor from H.D.U. came to see me and was pleased to see that I was coping better.

With the oxygen mask on, it made my lips very dry, which I think is very common but Ann had some lip salve which she put on my lips to stop them getting dry. Although feeling unwell, tired and a bit 'out of it' I still maintained the movements of my arms and legs which I was pleased about.

At 2pm, Pauline Spink arrived. I had met Pauline and her husband, Martin, at the church I went to when I first moved to Bristol. A really, lovely couple. She is a nurse herself and had just done a run of night duties at Southmead Hospital. She didn't realise that I was so unwell and told me that I didn't need to talk, just rest. Pauline stayed a short while and quietly sat next to my bed while I closed my eyes from feeling so tired. She was there one minute and gone the next. I appreciated people understanding that I wasn't well enough to talk and it wasn't a problem if I was quiet. Mum and Dad visited but I don't remember who brought them over from Chippenham. Dad said I looked very, very tired. He also said that I was breathing better – the oxygen mask had been removed by then. Both Mum and Dad said they loved me and that was precious to hear.

Later, around 4.30pm, Sue came to visit but I was asleep. Sue said that I didn't look particularly restful though. Sue mostly sat quietly so as not to wake me. I woke up at 4.45pm and Sue mentioned how busy and noisy the ward was today with lots of visitors but she said it made a change that they weren't crowding around my bed. I told Sue that I was feeling better but weary and still in some pain. At 5.25pm the noisy children that were around left, and peace and tranquility reigned again. Sue left at 5.30pm.

Eunice arrived at 7pm and was pleased to see me much better. Praise the Lord! Ruth and Will arrived at 7.45pm and were totally relieved to see a smile on my face. Ruth passed on Dave and Chris's love – who had phoned them just before their leaving home to come to visit me. Ruth and Will didn't stay too long but left me with some chocolates – me? Left alone with chocolates? No-one to accompany or supervise me? If anyone knows me well enough, they would know that I can't be left alone with chocolate.

WEEK FOUR

Thursday, 18th February 1999

Today I had a visit from a Speech Therapist. Why would a Speech Therapist visit me you ask? Well, because I was paralysed from the neck down it was possible that the muscles in my throat weren't working properly. She asked me to drink some water and swallow. She watched my throat and asked me to drink some more except this time she felt my neck as I swallowed. She tested some more and finally decided that I wasn't able to swallow properly. This meant that I would need a tube to be threaded down my nose into my stomach.

Ann came and I told her about the speech therapist. The speech therapist came back and said that I had to have a feeding– tube, I would be so gutted because I like to eat and taste my food. The physiotherapists came as well and brought a machine which was supposed to help expand my lungs. The machine had a tube for me to blow into, which was connected to this plastic, transparent casing with little coloured balls, and the idea was for me to blow as hard as I could to get the balls lifted. Fun but very hard work!

Ann gave me a bed bath which made me feel refreshed. You have no idea, Ann, how much better a patient can feel after a wash.

Eunice came with Emma and two people from her church at Alma Road, David and John. They prayed over me and David read a hymn about God caring for the future and John shared about the paralysed man at the Pool of Bethesda and that Jesus came to his aid when there was no one else.

In the meantime, Emma drew some pictures for me and wrote Emma and Mummy in my diary with lots of kisses. Emma has a good way of expressing her love for her Mummy! She loves cuddles and drawing loads of pictures with lots of love all over them.

Sue arrived later and, as ever, found something a little humorous to say. "One more tube than yesterday then! And don't worry about your hairstyle – *really*, it's fine!!" She encouraged me to keep wriggling my toes.

There were more people wanting to be in my 'bed gang'. After Sue, came Dave and Chris and I explained about my new sophisticated gadget with numbers on it - the Frentamat Enteral Feeding Pump, and I showed them my new trick of turning the light on and off. I think they were very impressed!

Friday, 19th February 1999

Ruth and Will arrived just after lunch when the nurses were trying to get me comfortable. I showed Ruth and Will the new gadget which was the F. E. F. Pump. Then a nurse came with some more painkillers through the feeding tube. Then antibiotics through the back of my hand and then Jo, the physiotherapist arrived to attack me while Ruth and Will went to the coffee shop. The Dietitian also arrived to work out the volume of mashed up food they were going to put through the feeding pump. Then Eunice came and she thought that I was looking better than I had done for a few days. I chatted to Eunice with regard to being down about the feeding tube. I'm not totally sure what was the problem and why I was so against the tube but it felt like a huge step backwards. To add to my discontentment, it made me feel sick so they had to give me some anti-sickness medicine to help.

Saturday 20th February 1999

Sue came and noticed that the curtains were drawn one side. This was mainly because of my noisy neighbour and my head was thumping. The nurses gave me 'Oramorph' but, sadly, it wasn't working.

Later, Eunice came and we wondered why my head was so bad. One suggestion was that it could be a withdrawal symptom from the lack of caffeine. I hardly drank coffee here which I missed. It was mostly water on the menu in this ward. Then Ruth and Will arrived but I think Ruth was upset to see me in such a state because she suddenly put her hand to her mouth and she was gone. But she did come back shortly afterwards so maybe she had gone to the loo. Apparently, Ruth had rung earlier to see how I was and she was told that I was improving and doing well. So, when Ruth arrived, she was shocked to see that I wasn't well and the headache had gone from bad to worse. I was flat on my back, feeling sick and Eun was trying to comfort me by smoothing her hand over the brow of my head, which did help a great deal.

Saturday night was another bad night and the oxygen mask was out again and lots of painkillers. I was given stronger painkillers and the bad head was beginning to ease but I was quite drowsy. Swallowing wasn't much better yet and I was getting very frustrated with myself.

Sunday 21st February 1999

Today I had a visit from Eunice and later Ruth, Will and Andy, which was lovely. Ruth suggested that I asked for a cup of coffee!!

My previous place of work, NMR in Chippenham had sent me a beautiful bunch of flowers. Andy was pleased to see that I had made a lot of progress since he first saw me when I couldn't move at all. This was a good reminder that I was moving forward and this made me smile. Andy talked about their new baby, Emily, and said she wants to meet her Aunty Chris very soon! Hurry up Chris, you don't want to meet her when she's starting school!

There was a young girl opposite me to the left called Sarah. She came over to me and introduced herself to me. She was at church the day she collapsed. Her legs gave way and she was numb from her waist down but she had been on another ward and by the time she came to this ward, she was walking but not very strongly. She was a very cheerful Sarah and I liked having her opposite me.

Monday, 22nd February 1999

Ann arrived to give me a bed bath – always welcome! The physios arrived to help me cough and to do some deep breathing exercises. After which I was put into a wheelchair, tubes and all! I said it was great to see the world from a different angle. Thankfully, the headache seemed to have gone. At last!

Dave and Chris arrived at 2pm and this time I was in the tilting bed again, but nearly vertical! The tilting bed and I aren't talking still, as there is some remaining friction between us. We may have to go for counselling together but 'flatbed' doesn't want to indulge in any conversation at all so I think it will be a waste of time and effort because we both must want this relationship to work!

I am trying to hold a pencil and pen to write again. It's painful but I can actually do it if I concentrate really hard and try and keep a steady hand.

Chris (Dave's Chris) wrote a verse in my diary today from ***Jeremiah chapter 31 verse 3:*** (New International Version)
"3 The LORD appeared to us in the past, saying; I have loved you with an everlasting love; I have drawn you with unfailing kindness."
Yes, He does love me and I should never forget that.

Eunice came when the Speech Therapist was checking me out again. She wasn't convinced that I was ready to lose the tube yet and said that it would be best to keep it in a little longer.

Sarah was going home today and she gave me her favourite verse in the whole Bible:

Jeremiah chapter 29 verses 11-13 (New International Version)
"[11]For I know the plans I have for you", declares the Lord, "plans to prosper you and not to harm you, plans to give you hope and a future. [12] Then you will call on me and come and pray to me, and I will listen to you. [13] You will seek me and find me when you seek me with all your heart".

She also wrote in my diary:

"It's been lovely being in the bed opposite you and seeing your smiling face each morning. It's good to see you improving day by day – and even sitting up in a chair today. Hang in there, and I'm sure you'll be jogging round Clifton before you know where you are! I hope that you continue to go from strength to strength and I will be thinking and praying for you lots sweetie pie. Bye for now, but I hope to see you again, lots of love and a big hug, Sarah XX"

She gave me her address and we did keep in contact for a while. The last I heard was that she was horse–riding, but her doctor was apparently quite cross with her and told her she shouldn't be doing such sports.

I was sleeping in the afternoon and feeling very tired and needed more pain killers for my back. I felt very dopey and was practically out of it when my friend Ali came to see me. She told me to carry on sleeping and left a teddy bear called Gracie. I love the name Gracie and her Mum's name was Grace and Martyn's Mum is also called Grace.

Each day was beginning to slip into the next and I almost felt institutionalised. The routine was much the same and the nights were mostly broken by about 4am with either noisy neighbours or head and back pain. If I couldn't go back to sleep, I would become really thirsty and it was a very, very long wait until the early morning tea and coffee round. So, by the time the trolley arrived I was desperate and just couldn't wait for that hot drink to start the day.

Tuesday, 23rd February 1999

Mum and Dad came and Dad shared that they had had several telephone calls asking how I was and saying how concerned they were and praying for me.

Eunice's friend David Cunningham (from her church in Clifton, Bristol) made a fleeting visit. He was a bit of a stranger to me but a friendly one and at least he didn't ask me to get in his car to give me a lift to school! Eunice must have only just missed him by minutes when she arrived. If she had known she would have been disappointed and would have kicked herself.

Wednesday, 24th February1999

It was gym this morning. Bryony said "We are going to stand you up today". I looked at her thinking she was a crazy woman or they were talking to the wrong patient – I really did! Bryony and Jo wheeled me to this wooden and leather strap frame. It looked like another piece of old-fashioned scaffolding from a dungeon. They proceeded to strap my ankles, legs, thighs, hips and waist to the 'climbing frame' and by the time they had belted my hips and waist I was standing up! I had no idea what muscles I needed to simply stand up; I felt I needed the muscles in my buttocks to keep me up – are they the main muscles you need to stand up? I have never thought about it before; you just stand up and sit down and take it for granted that it's something that you can do and not how or why. But I'm sure they were there somewhere trying to hold me up!

I had forgotten what the view looked like from up there! It was painful and I was very breathless but Bryony said I was doing really well and she stopped for a moment, looked up at me and said, very firmly, "Chris," you know you WILL walk again, don't you?" My reply was a simple "No" and I burst into tears. I just couldn't see it happening, but the fact that I was standing right now, ok with a lot of help and support, and Bryony was so positive and solid in what she said, I began to think that, maybe Bryony does know what's she's talking about and just maybe, just maybe, I will walk again.

Psalm Chapter 40 v 1-3

"I waited patiently for the LORD; and he inclined unto me, and heard my cry. 2 He brought me up also out of a horrible pit, out of the miry clay, and set my feet upon a rock, and established my goings. 3 And he hath put a new song in my mouth, even praise unto our God: many shall see it, and fear, and shall trust in the LORD."

Sue, Steve, Emma and Daniel came around 4.30pm and I told her the good news that I stood up today. She was very impressed and pleased for me. She tidied up around the bed- space which was getting a bit congested with, well, stuff. I had the table nearer me and had pen and paper to keep doing some hand physio by learning to write again. Sue's children were amusing themselves while Sue tidied up. I told Sue that I was having a twelve-hour break from the feeding tube but it was an odd feeling to drink water with a tube in your mouth and down your throat. Also, the drip was disconnected now so that was another development. My movements were getting better daily as I could sit up by myself with some effort, but I couldn't adjust the pillows on my own yet.

My friend, Mark, from Chippenham came in to see me and he said that the tube in my nose was almost as good as a nose stud. He was pleased to hear I stood up today and said to take it easy and concentrate on small steps for now.

Eunice came in with some work – lots of pigs to be drawn and cut out (for the church children's mission) – Ruth, Mark and Georgie (another visitor) helped out with these happy pig faces, which made short work of it all. Before Eunice left, I asked her to bring in some shoes and track suit bottoms if I could stand and get more mobile, I'll be able to get around but with proper clothes.

Ruth and Will came in with clean t-shirts for me and they were surprised that I was talking about shoes. I showed her a letter I had managed to write and she said that this was the progress that they had all been waiting for, prayers were being answered – after, what seemed to be a very long time!

21 The Fifth Week and Onwards

WEEK FIVE

Friday, 26th February 1999

Eunice noted that it was now five weeks since it had all begun and she had been sending out Progress Reports to friends and family. She had just finished the latest report and was showing me a photocopy of it. At that moment the Speech Therapist came and she said that my swallowing had improved but she was still not completely happy about removing the tube so I would have to wait until Monday when she would visit again and maybe then it could come out.

I actually woke up that day without a headache today which seemed the first since forever and it was such a relief. At the gym we were working on my arms. My arms were put in slings hanging from a bar and the idea was to swing my arms backwards and forwards as far as they would go. Another very painful exercise. "Ow-ow-ow!" Also, I stood up twice! I really felt that I was improving slowly. You just can't hurry these things and you need to be very, very patient with yourself. However, I'm not very patient with myself on things like this.

John and Penny came from Chippenham. They were really surprised that I looked so much better and my hair had been washed. John said that the physio must be doing me the world of good and that everyone at work was asking about me in their e-mails to him. He said that he would tell them that I was looking good and should be up and about soon. Penny said that it was great to see me again and was glad I was feeling better. She'd like to take me for a drink when I'm out and everyone at work sends their love. John and Penny were funny and very entertaining and always left a cloud of 'fun' behind them. Today, I wrote in the diary myself and this is what I wrote:

"Things just happen, don't they? Whether we are His children or not, things do happen to us. Life can be hard for some of us and nasty things do happen to us. That's life. But God is a God of love and I know He loves me and He's here with me helping me through this, watching me day and night. He knows the pain and frustration I'm going through and that's simple enough for me to take on board right now. – me, Chris".

By the time Ruth and Will arrived I was sitting in the wheelchair in casual wear, ready to go anywhere! Ruth said that people from BIME and Mum, Dad, as well as people from Ruth and Will's church, all sent their love. It's actually Mum's birthday today so I hoped she was eating cake! I drew a picture of a plate, knife and fork and wrote GONE TO LUNCH on it. Will got some Sellotape and stuck it to my Feeding Pump – Ruth liked that a lot, she thought it was funny.

At the gym I was progressing quite a bit now and Bryony and Jo were helping me to walk on the parallel bars. Well, not actually on them but my hands were on the bars. This was huge! The left leg was good but the right leg was lazy. And – guess what? – the nurses took away the ripple bed which was great news for me!

I could now get around more with the wheelchair by moving it myself with my hands which was an added physio task out of gym hours. Graham Vincent came and was impressed on how much I had improved. He said that the physios will have me running round the hospital grounds soon (but I honestly don't think so!).

I was sat in a wheelchair more and more and, because I had 'normal' but baggie clothes on because I had lost so much weight, I was thankful really because my leggings, sort of, hid my catheter bag, which was tied to my leg. But I was very conscious of it myself. Ann, Simon and James came to visit me briefly. I felt for the boys because it's a different and almost foreign world, here in the hospital. There's nothing for them to do and they probably just wanted to say hello and then go. They didn't stay long but it was lovely to see my nephews and I was grateful for their patience.

Eunice also popped in but I had had enough of being in the wheelchair as I was getting uncomfortable. Eunice didn't stay too long and shortly after she went the nurses put me back into bed.

Sunday, 28th February 1999

Joy and Emma (nurses) had a good sense of humour, so, I decided to have a bit of fun with them. When they were by my bedside, I complained about my left foot being swollen. They frowned and very gingerly went to touch it but I said "No – no- don't touch it, it will hurt!" As Joy's hand got closer to my 'swollen' leg she smiled and said "It's your catheter!" Of course, it was! I was having them on!

Then Eileen came over (another nurse) just at that moment and I said "Oh, we were just discussing my swollen leg." Eileen looked at my leg with widened eyes and said "Oh yes!" Again, I said "don't touch it though." (Both Emma and Jo played along). She went to put her hand out but soon realised it was my catheter bag. It was funny, we just burst out laughing because we had been so serious about it.

I had a bath this morning which was a lovely change from a shower. But it wasn't so easy because they used the crane to lift me up into it and I basically stayed in the sling of the crane. But at least I got my hair washed.

Eunice rang to say she was shattered and not able to come in today, which was fine by me. She deserved a rest. Coming in every day is a big ask to be honest. I should have told her earlier during this period of time that she didn't need to come in every day.

I telephoned Tim because I wanted to speak to Emma. She asked if I was better yet and I asked her what she wanted for her birthday next month. She wasn't sure but would think about it. Emma also said that she had made something for me but had left it at Grandma's. She said that she had a good time with Grandma, who lived in Croydon. I also spoke to Alex and asked him how he was, but all I got was heavy breathing down the phone and some gobble-d-gouch; bless him.

Ruth and Will arrived about 7.15pm and I had been in the wheelchair since 6pm. The evening's entertainment was Ros setting up my 'feeding bottles.' It wasn't straightforward but she managed it in the end. The next entertainment was that the auxiliary nurse came to empty my catheter bag. She came with the usual blue jug and it filled up to 700ml!!! The bag is only supposed to hold 500ml. I'm surprised the bag didn't break. The fuller the jug got the more our eyes got bigger and bigger with apprehension! We thought that there was going to be a big puddle on the floor. The nurse had clearly done this particular job before.

Monday 1st of March 1999

Mum and Dad came and my brother Tim. Mum and Dad were so pleased to see my progress and they said that they were so touched with all the phone calls that they were getting to ask how I was and to say that they were praying for me. Mum wrote in the diary before leaving that the doctors and team were very pleased with my progress and Mum wrote "and we are thankful to the Lord. Lots of love, Mum and Dad XX"

Brother Tim was really encouraged, on his first visit, to see for himself how much better I was (he lives in Eastbourne). He said that it reminded him of 'the God of all Hope'. He added that Rosalind and the children sent their love and they would continue to pray for me. While Tim was there, Eunice came. It was lovely to see them together, I'm glad their visits overlapped a bit. Eunice said that she felt better for the rest she had taken yesterday. (I think she's overdoing it). This afternoon, the tea trolley came along and interrupted my 'bed gang' and I asked for a coffee. This was my first coffee with the tube still in. Eunice wants to take me to the coffee shop, but is concerned that someone else might take me first.

Tuesday, 2nd March 1999

Sue came in today and Eunice and Emma as well. Emma drew in my diary but nothing much else happened today.

Wednesday, 3rd March 1999

I was a bit down this morning. Probably just tired. Eunice said that the doctor from A&E, Tim Burbridge happened to ring Chris Halfpenny and asked how I was. I was chuffed that he remembered me! This afternoon I was given a new friend: a Zimmer Frame. It was actually hard work on the arms but Eunice and I celebrated by going to the coffee shop – yey! We did it!

I am picking up as the day goes on. It seems funny now, that so many of the staff and visitors have got to know me and will stop to ask how I am and encourage me to keep going. I ask them in turn how they are doing, and it's surprising how many will sit on the edge of my bed or stand and talk about their current situations. I think I should have a consultation chair and a "de-stressing session". At 4pm, a lady called Christine Scott came back to the ward. She left on Monday to have a cyst removed from her brain. She came back to say she was shell-shocked. Today she was told that the cyst was cancer and terminal, there is no cure. They also told her that she had only two months to a year to live. She said that her doctor knows that she is a fighter and that she'll fight for longer. Christine was a gentle, soft-spoken lady who was clearly going through some troubles already. She had had a problem with her partner who was trying to control her. I told her to be strong and surely, she didn't want to live in that environment during her last months and the best thing she could do for herself and her older children was to get rid of him. She took this on board and said that she didn't know why she was still with him and she was going to be brave and ask him to leave.

We shared that we both had this amazing sense of someone carrying us through the illnesses. Chris told me that she couldn't explain it but I knew exactly what she was talking about. I asked her "Don't you think it's God?" and her reply was "Yes, I think so!"

A couple of days later she told me that she had asked her partner to leave but he wasn't very pleasant about it but her friends fully supported her. I didn't see her again after that.

7.20pm Sue arrived. I told Sue that I fancied a ride in the wheelchair to the dining room. Sue helped me by moving the chair next to the bed, which enabled me to stand up and step over to the wheelchair and sit in it. Sue was gob smacked! Then Ruth and Will came and saw me sitting at the dining-table which amazed them.

Thursday, 4th March 1999

WEEK SIX

HAPPY BIRTHDAY EUNICE! Have a big bubble bath, watch T.V., put your feet up and have a box of chocolates and RELAX. That was my message to Eunice today. Ann, Simon and Eunice came and we went into the dining-room and blew up three balloons for Eunice and had birthday cake. I think she really appreciated it.

Friday, 5th March 1999

Ted and Sally came in this morning even though it was their wedding anniversary, but it was lovely to see them. Then Ann came and I had a bath and then went to physio accompanied by Ann.

At 2.15pm Eunice, Mum and Dad, Ruth and Will came and we all went to the coffee shop. Although it was lovely to be around my family, I felt a bit odd. I think it had something to do with the wheelchair. People seem to think that you are really ill or that you can't hear or speak because you are in a chair on wheels. This is sad and it makes you feel very isolated or, at least, that's how it made me feel.

Dr Chris Halfpenny wrote in my diary. He said, "I am sorry it has been such a long haul for you. Your courage and good humour are an inspiration. It is an honour to look after you (if that is what I am doing). God bless, Chris". Underneath that, I wrote, "and I am really pleased that you are my doctor, yes, you are looking after me extremely well!! It's a pleasure to meet you and 'work' with you! God bless, Chris."

Ann (B), Bart (her husband), Shannon, Kerri and Connor came to see me, and the girls happily drew in my diary – mostly happy faces – and young Connor fell asleep in his pram. Ann was pleased that I was doing so well but was sorry that I had had a bad time.

Saturday, 6th March 1999

Sue, Daniel, Emma and Alex (who fell asleep) arrived at 2.05pm. I got out of the wheelchair into the armchair in the T.V. room and Emma gradually got more confident and chattier, bless her. I can't pick her or Alex up yet but I hope to soon. This was one of my aims – to pick up and cuddle my children again.

Andy and Kate came to visit. It's been four weeks since the arrival of baby Emily. They are both very happy, proud parents. I hope to meet Emily soon, just not sure when. Andy said that Mum was still in hospital in Bath. She has had three teeth out but because she is on warfarin, they had to be careful.

Sunday, 7th March 1999

Ruth and Will arrived after taking Mum and Dad back to Chippenham as Mum was discharged from the hospital today and they were pleased to be back home.

I think it was round about this time that the doctors and nurses decided to remove my catheter. I was quite worried about this and felt very insecure because I couldn't feel when I needed to empty my bladder. Apparently, I'll know and I should give it a go. I wore giant pads – not cricket pads either. My bladder had a mind of its own and only worked when it wanted to. For most of the day I thought I wanted to spend a penny and walked back and forth to the toilet just in case. This was a tough time and I didn't like it at all.

Monday, 8th March 1999

The speech therapist came to see if I could manage some mashed potato. I was determined to try my best *and* I must have done well because the feeding tube will be allowed to come out, but not today! But I think mashed potato is on the menu tomorrow as well.

Chris Halfpenny asked if I could speak to another patient, I can't remember her name, but she had just been admitted being paralysed from the waist down. He said if I could speak to her, she may be encouraged that she may be able to walk again. I found her, three beds down from me and tried speaking to her. But she wouldn't listen. I told her to give it time and that the doctors and nurses would do all they can to help her but there were so many negative vibes coming from her she practically pushed me away. I came away disappointed and feeling very sad for her.

By now, I was moving more and doing things for myself, like cleaning my own teeth and showering myself. I thought it was time to get out of here but I hadn't found any escape routes yet. But I had to get out soon as I was getting irritable and slightly stressed and stroppy inside. This was not a great feeling and I just wanted to be normal again, like, now. No patience there!

I struggled to read my Bible that Eunice had left on the table, because turning the pages wasn't easy and I had no concentration. So, I tried praying but my brain was here, there and everywhere. It's at times like these that you begin to doubt what you believe in and your faith wavers because you want to be heard and to know that someone is listening; you want your hand held and for someone to say "everything is going to be ok."

Faith is believing and faith is believing in something or someone you can't see. I sat silently, wondering how I was going to manage when I was allowed out, how would I pick up the children, will I ever drive again? All these questions buzzing around in my head. But you can't change some things and you have to find a different way forward. I chose to believe and have faith that God was there, I knew that the light shining through the string of cards above me at night was not letting me forget that He was watching over me; it's silly to go by your feelings, because one day they may be up and then, circumstances change the next day and your feelings are down. God is steady, He never goes away, it's me that's moving away by doubting.

Tuesday, 9th March 1999

My visitors today were Ann, Eunice and Alex. I was still working on walking and would try to Zimmer down the ward and back. The bladder wasn't working very well, but the feet and legs weren't doing too badly. Alex was a little unsure again on his arrival but he soon got used to me again. We went to the coffee shop and back which was fun. Then Alex attempted to eat a Jelly Baby and dribbled everywhere – it was so sticky and messy! I tried to kiss Alex good-bye but he didn't understand and then Eunice gave me a hug and kiss good-bye and he got the idea and came towards my face offering a kiss and a "bye-bye"! How cute!

Wednesday, 10th March 1999

Dr Chris Halfpenny was on his rounds this morning and I asked him when I could go home. He couldn't give a straight answer but he said he was happy with my progress and that he may have to keep me in to entertain everyone. But I told him that I do charge!!

Eunice came in with a real treat – 2 Aero chocolate mousses – and we ate them! And then Ruth and Will came and the pots were empty and we were licking our lips! The evidence was still on the table, we couldn't hide the Aero pots quickly enough. The thing is that I needed the chocolate for a boost of energy, you understand? I had been very busy tidying my table and sorting the in and out trays. The funny thing was that this happened during siesta time, and while I was standing between the table and bed I turned round and lost my balance. I fell flat onto the bed, feet still firmly on the floor but I was bent over the bed and I just couldn't budge an inch. I called out for help as I couldn't even touch the red button. Margaret, one of the auxiliary nurses came over and we had a giggle trying to get me back up. She suggested that I had done too much and my muscles had got tired. That should teach me, I should have been having my rest time! I didn't let that happen again – it was quite humiliating actually.

Thursday, 11th March 1999

WEEK SEVEN

Eun came with Emma today and they went to the shop to buy a Mother's Day card in the WRVS shop. They also went to the Café but it seemed as though they were closing so they couldn't stay very long. When Emma and Eunice came to see me in the Ward, they gave me a lovely Dairy Box of chocolate and I let Emma open it – it was another chocolate party – you can't go wrong with chocolate!

Emma drew me a lovely yellow flower in my diary and a picture of either me or Emma. Not sure which. But I showed Sue, who came in later and I don't think she could decide either. Sue also read about the chocolate box and was wondering where it had gone.

Friday, 12th March 1999

Well, this was a surprise – Melvin Bartlett came to visit me! I haven't seen him for years! He has such a humorous charisma, both Eunice and I lived with him and Mary (his wife) at different times in our lives – it was lovely to see him. After Mel, came Rachel, from Eunice's church, with fruit, magazines and hot cross buns, except they were cold of course. She was there one minute and gone the next though. Later that evening, Graham Vincent came in to visit again, which was nice.

Saturday, 13th March 1999

Sue arrived with her daughter Emma, my Emma and Alex, but I burst into tears when I saw Emma – I couldn't help it – she had had her hair cut short. She said she didn't like it and I was just stunned. But we all tried not to make a big thing of it and went into the dining room for a bit, then made our way down to the coffee shop and walked back to the T.V. room to see if there was anything on the television. Alex was very cuddly and Emma gave me lots of daisies, a Mother's Day card and a fluffy chick.

Eunice popped in briefly from her travels to Bournemouth, around 8.15pm, and while she was there Martyn rang, which was lovely too.

Martyn was allowed to come in later, after visiting-time, and he asked the nurses if he could take me out. They said that was fine as long as I was back by 10pm, or I would turn into a pumpkin! We didn't go far, just a short distance to a local pub. I felt a bit conspicuous and a bit like a naughty school girl, being out so late, or like someone who had escaped from jail! It was a lovely feeling to be out, even for a short while. I was nervous about falling over or not getting to the toilet in time. But Martyn was very careful, patient and caring which made it a lovely evening.

We got back in time for lights out and I was more than ready for bed; I just wanted to go to sleep. I had had all my tablets and I was feeling very tired and sick that night. Unfortunately, my noisy neighbour, Denise, who had been moved to the other end of the ward was being extremely loud and kicking out at the nurses which was really unfair of her. I was getting so irritated and wound up that my hackles were rising. It went on and on and everyone else was getting upset because they wanted to sleep as well. I exploded! I don't know what came over me – I couldn't help it and I shouted at the top of my voice and said "Denise!!!!!! Just shut up!" The ward went deadly silent. There wasn't another peak out of Denise that night. I felt bad really, it certainly wasn't like me to have an outburst like that, but it was all too much.

22 The Escape Plan Begins

Sunday 14th March 1999

Today, the staff nurse said that she heard about my outburst last night and maybe it would be a good idea to move me to a side ward where it would be much quieter. It was very posh! Almost like having a flat! Also today, Pearl, whose husband worked in the office for OMF came to visit me. But they couldn't find me as word hadn't got out yet that I had been moved, so they went all round the world and all the houses to find my side room. Pearl said that they went to get fresh air really! But she said that I was looking so much better and was smiling as usual and she didn't think it would be long before I was out.

Eunice came and said I looked better, especially in a side ward! She was allowed to bring a kettle next time, which would be good for the visitors as well. Then Ruth and Will came and found me too. Ruth called my room the "Keeper's Lodge," which she thought was luxury. She told me that Sarah from Croydon had rung to find out how I was, and then Ruth apologised for finishing the chocolates, but left lots of love instead.

Monday, 15th March 1999

Sue came to visit but thought I had gone 'AWOL' because she couldn't find me. Actually, I was just in the loo. Dave's Chris came at 4.30pm and she was surprised at the progress I had made since her last visit three weeks ago. And they celebrated with me because today they took my feeding tube out! This makes it closer to being set free!

Even more independence as Eunice came with a kettle and coffee. (More physiotherapy needed for lifting a kettle though – haha, my plans are working!).

At the gym today I was working on my getting up the stairs technique as well as getting up from the floor. Getting up from the floor was a lot harder than I thought but the stairs I could do as long as I could hold onto a rail. Also, they took me into a room to measure my right hand to make a cast to help straighten it out as they were concerned it would become claw- like. It was like the one they had made for my leg, but was for my wrist and hand. This was more painful to wear than you can imagine – ouch, ouch, ouch!

Tuesday, 16th March 1999

This was an exciting day as Eunice was going to take me out to Mothercare/Children's World *and* McDonald's Express. I was looking for a birthday present for Emma who would be 5 in a week's time. It was weird to begin with because I hadn't been out in the day time in a car for a long while and the cars were rushing past us so fast. I felt left behind and a strange feeling, a bit like motion sickness. I wanted Eun to drive slower but that could have been dangerous. But it was great to go out and do some shopping and I'm glad Eunice was there, as I wasn't confident yet.

This evening, Ruth and Will came while I was watching casualty. I think Ruth thought that the programme content was a bit close for comfort and probably, it was, but it was something to watch. Ruth wrote in the diary "Chris can do just about everything now. Out soon! Our prayers have been answered."

Yes, they have been answered, thank you Jesus. Who would have thought, on the 28th January, with no movement from the neck down, I would be in this position now? Ok, I couldn't quite pick up things and walk straight, etc. but I was walking, breathing better, swallowing and sitting better – lots of better! So, my plan of escape was coming together!

WEEK EIGHT

Thursday, 18th March 1999

Eunice came with Emma and Alex. Emma was a bit whingey today (maybe she was having an off day?), but Alex was very chatty, whatever he was saying, it's good to talk.

The staff suggested that I had a trial of going home for a night – a sleep-over – on Saturday. I liked the sound of that but was also scared. I couldn't cope with the bladder problem; I just couldn't control it and it was not only embarrassing but also distressing. Some days I would sit in the loo and just cry. Thankfully, before I went for my overnight stay, they started me on Oxybutynin to help relax my muscles around the bladder. I did think that I had all the help I needed here, so why do I need to go? But, hang on, thinking like that is going against my plan to get out of here. This could be good for me, couldn't it? 'Stop worrying Chris' I said to myself.

Friday, 19th March 1999

What a lovely surprise – Andy *and* Mark came to visit me today. We chatted about going for a sleep-over on Saturday, and Andy called it D-Day and suggested that, by then, I would be fitter than the rest of them, I'm not sure why though. Maybe Andy wasn't feeling well himself? (Kate and baby Emily sent their love anyway). We walked around the hospital grounds. The weather was warmer than the day I came here and the daffodils were out in full bloom, loads of them and looking blooming marvellous.

Eunice and I popped over to Tesco's this afternoon – I wish those cars would slow down; they are going far too fast! Surely, they are way over the speed limit!?

The Speech Therapist wrote in my diary, "A very delightful and conscientious patient. Always a smile on her face. I will keep you in my mind as an example for me and for the others. With lots of love."

And nurse Joy wrote, "This is Joy, the nervous nerve nurse who is not sure what to write. I have enjoyed watching your personality emerge from behind the pillow. It's a shame you can't come skiing with me next week but perhaps you are not quite up to it yet. Lots of love, Joy (with the nice shoes)"

Saturday, 20th March 1999 – D-DAY

D-Day as Andy put it. Going home went better than I expected. But both Eunice and Martyn were very kind and didn't push me too hard; I didn't have to do too much either, just remember to take all the tablets that I was on and try and adjust to being out of hospital.

Going back to Frenchay was very difficult. I didn't want to be there because I wanted to get on with life. I realised how institutionalised I had become which isn't a good place to be in. I got more irritable and frustrated but they gave me tablets to help calm me down. It's 'me' really, trying to adjust to what I could and couldn't do and I didn't know what was ahead of me in this condition of not being fully recovered or 100%. I wasn't sure if I'll ever be me again and the medical staff didn't know either.

By Monday, 22nd March 1999 I was officially out! I was free from the routine of hospital life. I was given some lovely farewell wishes, handshakes, hugs and bags of medication!!

23 Getting on with Life

Being back home wasn't easy. There were loads of things that I discovered I couldn't do. I couldn't cook, I *could* turn taps on but I couldn't turn them off. Getting to the loo wasn't easy as the stairs were awkward and I kept thinking I need a wee and when I did, I couldn't go and when I didn't think I need to go, it was too late. So, a very challenging time. My tablets were spread out on the table and I had to sort them out into days as some of them I didn't need to take daily as they were weaning me off some of them especially the steroids. My brain was a bit 'spongy' so I needed help with sorting them out.

Time went from days, to weeks and months. I moved into a flat in Bristol and about seven months later moved back to my home town of Bath. I was getting stronger, physically and mentally – my brain wasn't so spongy anymore. I had learnt to drive again – not easy with the changing gear as my left hand was still painfully stiff and didn't like moving the gear stick, but I managed with Martyn's help and an empty car park!

It has been a long road and an extraordinary one. Years ago, when I was younger, I thought that life was boring and that nothing happened in my life. That's certainly not true anymore.

It has taken years to walk better, breath better and for the numbness to wear off. I am now only numb in patches around the trunk of my body. My right foot still drops and I can't hold things for very long, or stand for any length of time and the bladder still doesn't work, only with medication. Headaches and migraines come often as well as aching limbs, spasticity, tiredness, ribs and back ache. Wearing sensible foot wear is important because for a couple of years my feet felt weird walking on carpets and cold floors, a sensation that I can't really explain. But over time my feet now feel normal but my sense of balance isn't very good. I also have Fibromyalgia to cope with. But I have learnt to live with it all and manage the pain as best I can and I certainly appreciate the good days, the times when I feel well and can walk. Some mornings I would wake up and struggle to get out of bed. On those off days I just stay there until I can face getting up and going downstairs. Sometimes, I would just stay in my pyjamas, put my feet up and rest. Walking again is a huge blessing for me and my heart goes out to people using wheelchairs, frames or sticks, because they should be listened to, we should include them – they are human beings just like me and you. So often I felt like people thought I couldn't hear or speak for myself.

Martyn's family gave me a warm reception. I got to know his Mum and Dad for about seven years before they were both called home to be with Jesus. He also has three lovely, older sisters, all who are Christians and have lovely, warm hearts. Ann is his eldest sister, married to Malcolm Steer and Hilary is his second eldest sister who is married to Malcolm's brother Graham Steer! Two brothers married two sisters, which has a wow factor! And Martyn's third, and youngest sister is Rose, who is married to Dave Edgar and lives in New Zealand. They have certainly given us much love, prayer, advice and support over the years and we love them very much.

Martyn was the youngest of the family and although his mum had been made sterile, she still became pregnant with Martyn five years after Rose was born. He is truly a miracle!

Martyn and I did get together and got married 10th June 2000. Emma and Alex came to live with us in Bathampton, Bath. Emma was about 6 and Alex 4 when they moved in with us. They made some lovely friends from Bathampton Primary School. A lovely village school by the canal.

The school always needed help with reading, the library, school trips and dinner ladies and I joined in with these things. Later I went to college in the evenings to get my Teaching

Assistant certificate, Level 2. It was hard work because the amount of written work was huge and going to college in the evening was my tired part of the day and I often found myself dozing off! Also, it added to the average daily headaches that I was already experiencing. But I got there and was able to work at Bathampton Primary as a Teaching Assistant in Emma's class as well as Alex's. It was great fun!

Martyn and I also set up our own business in 2000, a car repair garage which eventually became an MOT station as well. Martyn often says "Individually, we are good as a team!"

Running the garage together was very hard work. I had to learn to do Tax Returns and to keep on top of the legal documents such as different licenses that were required under MOT regulations, PAYE and the list goes on.

In early 2006 we were burgled. I am sure many readers have had this experience, it's very intrusive and upsetting. We were about to go out to the park and Emma had just given me all her birthday money and savings – she said that she wanted to help us buy a house. It was over £100.00, bless her! Because we were about to go out, I thought I would give it back to her when we return and would tell her that I wanted her to use her money for something she really wanted. Alex didn't have any cash but had a large, red money box with a lock and key. It was very heavy but not with coins. What he had put in were decorative glass pebbles; they were shiny and beautiful to him. When we returned from the park, we discovered that the intruders had found Emma's money and also thought they were onto something when they found Alex's money box. It was in the downstairs hallway and they had prised it open and the shiny pebbles were spilled out over the floor.

This experience pushed us to seriously look for a house to buy and we counted up our savings and found that we actually did have enough to buy a house. Later that year, 2006, we moved into our new home in Trowbridge, Wiltshire. A lovely house that looked onto a meadow with deer, and occasionally badgers and foxes.

Chip was our new addition to the family in October 2006. A tri-colour Jack Russell who was my little boy and got me walking more and more. He would always sense when I was having a bad day and would lie next to me for several hours patiently waiting to go outside. He loved rabbit and badger holes. If it was a good day, I would treat him to an extra-long walk along the edge of the fields we took him to and he would spend ages sniffing around the tree roots and rodent holes in the ground. He was a very loyal, funny and loving dog.

Chip wasn't really allowed on the furniture or upstairs even! But I spoilt him by letting him sit on my lap or curl up next to me if I was sitting watching the television or reading and I would let him upstairs too! He would always wait on the bottom of the stairs and wait for me to give him permission to come or he would listen for my whistle and he would run up to find me! He realised that Martyn was the one who didn't like him on the furniture or allow him to come up stairs so he learnt that as soon as Martyn left for work in the mornings and the door was shut, he would race upstairs and snuggle next to me. It did mean that I had to keep brushing off the dog hair from the bed covers though! One morning Martyn shut the door, Chip ran up and got under the duvet, but then Martyn came back in and upstairs because he had forgotten his watch. Thankfully, he was in such a hurry and didn't see the bump next to me under the duvet. Chip stayed snuggled and I had a chuckle as Martyn left the house not knowing where Chip was!

Emma and Alex have grown up now and have lives of their own. Emma and her partner Joe having two gorgeous little girls, Evelyn and Alessia, and Alex is engaged to an American girl, Brittany. But I love recalling memories of going to Bristol Zoo, Lego Land, Euro Disney, Longleat and so on. Once when we were going to Longleat, Emma asked if she could go on a 'stimulator', meaning the simulator machines that they had at Longleat. Also, Alex became interested in cars and he could identify them by their badges. He particularly liked the Mercedes cars and called them 'spy cars'! He also said that when he grew up, he would want a Safari car, meaning a Ferrari! Bless them!

Returning to the garage, Martyn worked hard and occasionally long hours, gave personal attention and kept a high level of good, quality work. There were always the worries of the overheads. I am sure other people running their own businesses would understand. We had some lovely customers and some odd ones and others were comical characters. We had one, called Barry. He was quite a character and always brightened up our day. He used to come in with some funny stories.

In one story in particular, Barry was driving along a road in Wiltshire and an accident happened ahead of him. Nobody was hurt but the car in front had rammed into a lamp post. The lamp post was broken to the ground so the car must have hit the post with quite some force. As Barry drove home he thought to himself "Mmmmm….. I fancy a lamp post in my garden." So later that night Barry returned to the crash scene with a pair of pliers to cut the cables of the damaged and very sad looking lamp post (how he didn't electrocute himself we just don't know!). Took it home and connected it up in his kitchen. He said "Wow, Mart. The light from it was so bright it was too much!" He decided it was definitely better to put his adopted lamp post into his back garden. We are sure it could be seen from outer space, it stood out like a 'sore thumb' every time we passed his house! And they lived happily ever after, well, until he moved house that is.

Martyn and I started going to Bethesda Baptist Church in Trowbridge. Martyn started to help with the Soup Run, providing hot soup at night for the homeless people in the town. He loved the work and really had a heart for the homeless. He read a book called "One Step Beyond", by Gram Seed and then his second book, "It Must Be Love". Gram had had a rough life of being a down and out, but by God's amazing love and grace was healed out of a near-death crisis situation. Gram's books gave Martyn a bigger heart for the destitute.

24 Walking for Gram Seed

The "Men United" Christian group in Trowbridge organised a Men's Breakfast every couple of months and Martyn was thrilled when he found out, at one of those breakfasts, that Gram Seed was coming to town! It was arranged that he would come for the whole weekend, and Martyn and I organised with others for Gram to speak in the town park. We didn't realise how much red-tape there was to sort out with the council and the P.A., music and, of course, making it known that Gram was coming.

On the day, the weather wasn't very good and we all ummed and ahhed over whether it was a good idea to go ahead with "Meet Gram in the Park", as the weather was so wet. But Martyn was sure it was God's purpose to have the meeting in the park and not inside the church. Amazingly, the sun came out in time and Gram, who had been walking around the town centre, appeared like the Pied Piper with a string of youngsters behind him before the meeting began. From that day on, we have stayed good friends with Gram, giving prayer support to his ministry and his wife, Natasha, and boys, Caleb and Boaz.

We wanted to help Gram financially and thought it would be good if we could raise some money for his ministry. The only thing I felt I could do was to do a sponsored walk. We trained by doing lots of different walks, as I needed to become stronger and to be able to walk further than the usual walk round the field with Chip.

The first sponsored walk for Gram, Martyn did without me as I wasn't up to it yet. Martyn joined some friends and walked the Yorkshire Three Peaks, Pen-Y-Ghent, Whernside and Ingleborough. It was an exhausting 20-hour walk but he did it even though he got split up from his group and nearly got lost!

We stayed at a Premier Inn overnight but I woke up coughing and not being able to breath properly. Martyn dragged himself out of bed when all he wanted to do was sleep. He took me to the nearest hospital but they couldn't find anything wrong. I had several of these attacks where my windpipe or trachea felt closed and I was not able to breath properly. After some tests it was later discovered that I had Whooping Cough! It can be frightening but, thankfully, I did recover.

Martyn took a while to recover from the Three Peaks, and decided that he probably would not do such a difficult walk again; but he did love the challenge and he raised over £1,000.00 for Gram!

For several years after the Three Peaks Challenge, we got ourselves prepared for other sponsored walks, and some I could join in with. We walked all the way around Portland Island; we have walked from West Bay to Golden Cap with our friends Karen and Gareth Hopkins. Martyn walked the Imber Path with his friend Alan Ridout, which is a 30-mile round trip. Martyn walked up and down Snowdon with Karen and Gareth and I met them at the top by travelling on the Mountain Railway.

Another time, Martyn, Alan, and his wife Margaret, decided to do a sponsored walk to the top of Snowdon again, but via Crib Goch, which has a knife-edge ridge. It looks dangerous and Martyn doesn't like heights! I was truly scared for Martyn's safety for this trip, and as I got on the mountain railway to meet them at the top I just hoped and prayed that they would make it. A couple of hours later I was amazed to meet all three of them at the summit café.

Martyn took me aside and told me that they had actually missed the turn off for the trail to Crib Goch – Paise the Lord!, I thought. But Martyn was concerned because people were paying or sponsoring him to walk that knife-edge, so he asked if I would be willing to walk down with them but on the Miners' Path, which would count as a stiff challenge, but isn't as difficult as Crib Goch. Martyn knew that I couldn't tackle that knife-edge walk (and neither could Margaret because she had hurt her back). Oh, my goodness, I thought! I wasn't prepared for this. But after some thought and persuasion, I decided to give it a go. It was much further than I expected and there were some very steep and slippery rocks, but with a great deal of care I did it and I was really, really impressed with myself.

The last sponsored walk we did was with our dear friend Anthony Oliver, Wilhelmina (or Willy as she is known - my sister-in-law) and Hannah (my niece). We walked the Pen-y-Fan Horseshoe ridge hiking trail, which is about 8.5 miles. The views were beautiful but it was a difficult trek. Some of it was steep and it was a very hot day and it was further than I expected, it felt like 20 miles to me!

Although we are unable to do so much walking now, as Martyn suffers with back problems as well, we keep in good contact with Gram. We encourage each other on our different walks of life.

25 Moving Forward

Martyn loves taking photographs and wherever we go and whatever we are doing he likes to capture those moments. We have an amazing collection of photos – too numerous to count but we often look through the albums and we have quite a multitude of memories together. We have come so far and have done so much, partly, because Martyn lives a life of significance and meaning. He has a lovely laugh, he is very encouraging, cares for others and loves Jesus.

Now I can look back over the last 24 years since going down with Transverse Myelitis and I have come a long way. It is true that time is a healer, whether of physical or emotional damage. Sometimes I think being in a wheelchair can be less painful than some of the heartache I have experienced, which in many ways doesn't sound right.

We have enjoyed some lovely holidays and trips away. And we are grateful for those times, we needed those times. Taking time away from the stresses of business and life has given us times of blessing. We have had many holidays in Cornwall with children; we have travelled to France, Holland, Spain, Scotland, by road and plane, Rome, Venice and Florence. Beautiful, beautiful places and great memories.

In life, when you can have those times out, it can be like going up a hill and getting a different perspective on things. When you are stuck in the lowlands and are continually trudging through life in difficult times, you need refreshing.

After twenty years of running the business in Batheaston, Bath, we finally closed it 31st August 2021. After the Covid Lockdown, business life became more and more stressful and we have got older; we aren't as young as we were and Martyn's back told him so!

Don't take life for granted, but live each day with love for each other and be quick to forgive. God has been with us in all the ups and downs that life has thrown at us. He has been right next to us all the way. Life is about Love. Loving Jesus and others, and Jesus loving us.

26 Transverse Myelitis

This is my understanding of Transverse Myelitis as I experienced it.

Transverse Myelitis often occurs after a virus infection, and has been described as an autoimmune disease. When the immune system breaks down the body can't cope with any more illness; so, with the next infection that comes along Transverse Myelitis can arise. It's an inflammation on each side, or across the spinal cord in one area. But there are, of course, other causes for this illness. Only 1 in 8 million people fall victim to T.M. each year.

This inflammation interrupts the nervous system, and the location of the swelling – how high up or low down in the spinal cord – determines the loss of movement and messages to the brain.

Because my spinal cord was infected in sections C1 and C2, the paralysis was from my neck down. The messages from my brain could not get through to my legs to walk or arms to move, nor could I go to the toilet or feel hot or cold. It doesn't mean that your organs stop working, you just have to think of it that your muscles and the 'outside' (skin deep) has been numbed.

As soon as is possible, the best treatment is steroids as well as physio. Steroids to reduce the swelling and physiotherapy to remind your limbs how they used to work. Unfortunately, it's not going to go overnight and much depends on the damage already done before the steroids are administered.

There is a great deal of pain that comes with this and there are different medications to help manage the discomfort. Sometimes, I just want to sleep the struggles off but other times you need perseverance and patience with yourself.

Patience will help you to get through the healing process; make some weekly goals, don't get down with any setbacks you might face, and grapple and confront those huge hurdles. Somethings just don't happen overnight.

I was given 33% chance of recovery, and when you are told that, you feel you haven't got much chance at all. But I would encourage you to fight this battle and you'll find that you are not the only one - Transverse Myelitis on Facebook is a good "place" in which to encourage each other and ask questions. Also, be prepared to accept and learn new talents and skills if, for example, those legs won't do what you want them to do. I say this because at one point I did feel I had to face and be real at the prospect of being in a wheelchair for the rest of my life: but it is really not the end of the world – it's a new challenge.

Printed in Great Britain
by Amazon

21403713R00099